race • **Birch Bayh** • Green Bea... ...Beef Borscht • Spaghetti
...• Chicken & Brandy • Blender H... Lobster • **J. Carter Brown**
...y Buchanan • Chicken Piccata ... ...s • Pineapple Upside-Down
...r Burns • Veal Piccata • Omel... ...• Old-fashioned Apple Pie •
...tcake • **John Chancellor** • Baco... ...Basque
...on • French Brioche • Sour Cream Fudge Cake • **Clifton**... ...auce •
...Batter • Zucchini Salad • Chocolate Mousse • **Antal Dora**... ...quash
...m Loaf • **Barry Goldwater** • Black Walnut Stew • **Robert Griffin** • Meat Sauce for
...erstam • Ham & Clam Chowder • Lamb in Marinade • Clay Pot Chicken • **H. R. Haldeman**
...nouj • Tabbouleh • Maqloobeh • Mensef • **Henry Jackson** • Nordic Loaf Cake • **Jacob**
...h & Shrimp • Eggplant Stuffed with Shrimp • Shrimp Creole • Okra & Tomato • Blackberry
...ils • Keeley's Egg Salad & Keeley's Fried Egg Sandwiches • Tomato Quiche • Mauritian
...nder • Pasta with Clam Sauce • Bread • **Aaron Latham** • Ham & Cheese Poker Chips
...m Cheese Frosting • **Robert McClory** • Swiss Cheese Fondue • Sour Milk Pancakes
...tte Pasties • **Gillespie Montgomery** • Marinated Mushrooms • Lemon Pepper Melbas
...on Bread • Ambrosia • Bourbon Coffee Ice Cream • **Patrick Moynihan** • Lasagna alla
...llions with Fried Pork • Grilled Leg of Lamb • Chinese Chicken Wings • Fried Chicken with
...k Steak • **William Proxmire** • Fruit Salad • **Dan Rather** • Brisket of Beef with Sauce
...n with Wine & Vinegar • Green Sauce • Caramel Mousse • **Stewart Richardson** • Roast
...ghetti • **Peter Rodino** • Escarole Soup • Veal with Marsala • Fried Italian Peppers • Fried
...colate Roll • **William Safire** • Steak Tartare • House Dressing for Green Salad • May Wine
...d Zucchini Strips • Upside-Down Apple Tart • Caramelized Orange Slices • **Dan Schorr**
...t au Gratin • **Senate Dining Room** • Bean Soup • Beef Birds with Sauce • **William Shannon**
...Stevens • Poached Sable Fish • Chocolate Fondue • **Stuart Symington** • Bul Go Gi
...rmond • Crab Cakes • **John Tower** • Chili • **John Tunney** • Indonesian Rice • **James**
...k Tartare • Boned Venison Sirloin • **Warren Weaver** • Liver Pâté Normandy • Eggplant
...nian Rice • **White House Chef** • Green Sauce • **Tom Wicker** • Pot-roasted Beef Lamande
...liams • Shrimp Mousse • **Russell Baker** • Veal Scallopini • Chicken with Cream & Tarragon
...eef Borscht • Spaghetti with Basil & Tomato Sauce • Banana Ice Cream with Sour Cream
...bster • **J. Carter Brown** • Cold Avocado Soup • Special Graham Crackers • Meringue Cake
...Pineapple Upside-Down Cake • **Art Buchwald** • Lamb and Parsley Stew • **James Buckley**
...oned Apple Pie • Applesauce Cake • Apple Crisp • **Jimmy Carter** • Peanut Soup • Eggplant
...ch • Basque Chicken • **Craig Claiborne** • Meat and Spinach Loaf • Southern Fried Chicken
...Sauce • Turkey or Chicken in Cream • Cold Poached Salmon with Sauce Gribiche • Shrimp
...sh with Dill • **David Eisenhower** • Pan-fried Steak • Hot Fruit Salad • Cheese Grits • **John**
...aghetti • Stuffed Peppers • Pancakes with Beer & Blueberries • Danish Crescents • **David**
...estern Omelet • **Hubert Humphrey** • Beef Soup • **King Hussein** • Hummus al Tahini • Baba
...its • Stuffed Cabbage • **Bennett Johnston** • Jambalaya • Green Peppers Stuffed with
...• **Robert Keeley** • Chicken with Vermouth & Black Cherries • Mauritian Fish • Mauritian
...tney • Pineapple Meringue Tart • **Edward Koch** • Gazpacho • **Ned Kenworthy** • Sautéed
...oli Soufflé • **Paul Laxalt** • Basque Soup • **Anthony Lewis** • Granola • Carrot Bread
...liam Macomber • Shepherd's Pie • **Frank Mankiewicz** • Lentil Soup • **Mike Mansfield**
...ck-eyed Peas with Hog Jowl • Chicken Parmesan • Corn Pudding • Bacon-wrapped Beans
...ognese • Green Spaghetti • Omelette aux Fines Herbes • **Gaylord Nelson** • Sour & Hot Soup
...nuts • Bananas Flambé • Brownie Pie • Sweet and Sour Pork • **Robert Packwood** • Marinated
...mes Reston • Mince • Eggs Fulton • **William Rice** • Grilled Kidneys & Sweetbreads
... Prince Orlov • Foil Pot Roast • Vichy Carrots • **Cliff Robertson** • Mussels • Clam Sauce for
...chini • **Kenneth Rush** • Sea Bass with Fennel • Scallops en Brochettes • Brussels Fondue
...s Souci • Cold Rabbit in Terrine • Chicken from the Auge Valley • Fried Zucchini Flowers
...r & Onions • Charlotte Malakoff • **Richard Schweiker** • Shrimp Dip • **Hugh Scott** • Cra
...Bexar County Bean Casserole • Brioche • **Herbert Stein** • Leg of Lamb • Veal Shanks Stein
...man Talmadge • Baked Country Cured Ham • Garlic Grits • Cucumber Mousse • **Stron**
...berg • Hot Borscht • Cheese, Tomato, & Sour Cream Omelet • **Malcom Wallop** • Wyoming
...ognese • Polish Hunter's Stew • Chicken Tetrazzini • Chicken Breasts • Squaw Corn
...mp & Pesto Sauce for Spaghetti • Eggs Sardou • Hollandaise Sauce • Cheesecake • **Harrison**
...téed Scallops • Orange à l'Arabe • **Birch Bayh** • Green Bean Casserole • **Carl Bernstein**

GUESS WHO'S IN THE KITCHEN?

If there's any truth to the saying that you are what you eat, then here's a book that offers some tantalizing revelations about some of the world's most powerful and influential men: what they like to eat!

Kathryn Wellde, a gourmet cook and long-time resident of Washington, D.C., has combined her culinary skills with her inside know-how and has gathered favorite recipes from senators and congressmen, journalists, ambassadors, and kings. The result is an extraordinary cookbook, spiced with the comments of the contributors, and Mrs. Wellde's own comments about the recipes. The items range from the exotic—Mensef, a dish that calls for an entire roasted lamb, from the Court of King Hussein of Jordan—to more down-to-earth fare — David Eisenhower's Pan-fried Steak. There are regional American specialties: Peanut Soup (from Plains, Georgia), Shrimp Creole (Louisiana), Barry Goldwater's Black Walnut Stew, the Moynihans' homemade pasta. Mrs. Wellde also canvassed the international circuit for such delicacies as Sea

(continued on back flap)

(continued from front flap)

Bass with Fennel from the French Embassy, Roesti from the Embassy of Switzerland, Italian ice cream. But she did not overlook traditional Washington favorites, including the Senate Dining Room's Bean Soup, and gourmet recipes from the owner of Sans Souci.

Organized with sections for appetizers and soups, entrees, vegetables, breads, desserts, and beverages, GUESS WHO'S IN THE KITCHEN? begins with an introduction by Mrs. Wellde and a delightful foreword by Tom Wicker. This is a personal book, a collector's book, which promises good eating, good reading, and plentiful amusement.

GUESS WHO'S IN THE KITCHEN?

Kathryn Wellde

Illustrations by Vida Rouse

DOUBLEDAY & COMPANY, INC., GARDEN CITY, NEW YORK   1979

Grateful acknowledgment is made to the following sources:

"Ham and Clam Chowder" and instructions for steaming clams from *Love, Thyme and Butter,* by Joe Hyde. Copyright © 1971 by Joe Hyde. Reprinted by permission of Richard W. Barron Publishing Co., Inc.

"Bongo Bongo Soup," by Victor J. Bergeron. Reprinted by permission.

"Sea Bass with Fennel," "Scallops en Brochette," "Brussels Fondue," and "Roulé Marquis" from *Le Cookbook,* by Chef Robert Bolard.

"Polish Hunter's Stew" ("Bigos"), by Michael Field, from *Michael Field's Cookbook.*

"Green Sauce" (originally titled "Sauce Verte") by Henry Haller, appeared in the Washington *Post,* June 10, 1976. Reprinted by permission.

"Shrimp Fried in Beer Batter," "French Brioche," "Sour Cream Fudge Cake," and excerpt from p. ix in *The New York Times Cook Book,* edited by Craig Claiborne. Copyright © 1961 by Craig Claiborne. "Southern Fried Chicken" in *The New York Times International Cookbook,* by Craig Claiborne. Copyright © 1971 by The New York Times Company. Reprinted by permission of Harper & Row, Publishers, Inc., and John Schaffner Literary Agency.

"Pot-roasted Beef Lamandé" from *Clémentine in the Kitchen,* copyright © 1963 by Samuel Chamberlain. Used by permission of Hastings House, Publishers.

Quotes by Craig Claiborne, November 9, 1975; "Coulibac de Salmon," by Craig Claiborne, December 27, 1976. Copyright © 1975, 1976 by The New York Times Company. Reprinted by permission.

"Meat and Spinach Loaf" from *Craig Claiborne's Favorites from The New York Times,* Vol. 1, by Craig Claiborne. Copyright © 1975 by The New York Times Company. Reprinted by permission of Quadrangle/The New York Times Book Co.

"Shrimp and Pesto" from *Italian Family Cooking,* by Edward Giobbi. Copyright © 1971 by Edward Giobbi. Reprinted by permission of Random House, Inc.

The author wishes to thank Mrs. Adrianne Burk of the New York *Times* Washington Bureau, who helped edit this book.

Designed by Laurence Alexander

Library of Congress Cataloging in Publication Data
Main entry under title:

Guess who's in the kitchen?

Includes indexes.
1. Cookery. I. Wellde, Kathryn.
TX652.G83   641.5
ISBN 0-385-13374-X
Library of Congress Catalog Card Number 77-82776

Copyright © 1979 by Kathryn Wellde

This cookbook is dedicated to my five children:

George
Michael
Kristen
Jennifer
Philip

who made it nearly impossible for me to complete.

Foreword

In early cooking days—that is, before experience settled in—I used to waste hours looking through cookbooks. Many are written as an encyclopedia to be studied, and I remember being discouraged at the multitude of recipes to sort through before finding an exciting one.

One of my reasons for putting together this cookbook is that each recipe yields a delicious dish, and there are not so many as to boggle the mind.

This is a compendium of recipes from prominent professional men who like to cook and like to eat. They are diplomats, politicians, businessmen, government executives, and men in the media. Some are well known *because* of their culinary achievements.

Many of the cooks who have shared their recipes have busy wives who work away from home or enjoy the public limelight with them. The husbands are obliged to help at home and admit that they would rather cook than clean, baby-sit, or tackle other household chores. Cooking is relaxing and sociable, they say, and it certainly is the only creative part of housekeeping.

The interviews reveal that gourmet cooks are mainly interested in preparing one delicious, usually time-consuming, main course. A caring cook will not devote time to side dishes or first courses that detract from his masterpiece, for if he has planned, shopped, peeled, chopped, and coaxed together a beautiful paella, for example, he does not want the appetite dulled with filling hors d'oeuvres. And *after* the paella feast, there is no space for dessert.

However, the American sweet tooth must be catered to and some delicious dessert recipes have been provided. And appetizers have their place with that necessary panacea, the cocktail.

Young men are the more innovative cooks. They enjoy working in the kitchen and speak freely about improvisation with recipes, with no inhibitions about their cooking ability. Older men, while they are careful not to actually say so, feel that the preparation of food is "woman's work," and the recipes from the over-fifties are often omelets or something on the back yard barbecue grill.

This is especially true with many of Washington's foreign diplomats. It must be difficult for a man who is always referred to respectfully as "His Excellency" (often the words Ambassador Extraordinary and Plenipotentiary follow his name) to admit that he cooks. This job is usually a lowly one in his native country and is nearly always done by menials and women. Menials *or* women is probably the way it is. But they readily admit that attitudes as well as practice are slowly changing in the home country.

GUESS WHO'S IN THE KITCHEN? is of international flavor because most American dishes (as well as most Americans) have their origins in other countries. We have also had more exposure to foreign travel, and many have tasted the sauces of France and the pastas of Italy. It is interesting to note that the buying and eating habits of Americans have changed considerably in the last decade. Exotic foreign ingredients are available in most city supermarkets and Julia on TV makes the blending of *sauce béarnaise* seem like "Child's" play.

K.W.

Washington, D.C.
March 1978

CONTENTS

Introduction by Tom Wicker

Cooking is the vice of my middle age. It tasks me, it heaps me, as Ahab said of the White Whale; and I pursue it not exactly with maniacal fury but with more zeal than my waistline, cholesterol count, and office hours can accommodate. I find myself poring over recipes as once I studied the federal budget. I browse through housewares emporia as in my intellectual youth I haunted bookstores. Instead of pondering Jimmy Carter's share of the black vote, I memorize the conversion ratios, teaspoons to tablespoons, cups to pints, etc. I once spent an entire afternoon trying to find cane syrup for pecan pie in New York, I have had country ham flown in by air mail from Tennessee, and just recently, to a perfect stranger on the subway, I said pugnaciously: "Why do *all* Craig Claiborne's recipes call for heavy cream?"

No doubt about it, I'm hooked. My wife, Pamela, and I give each other expensive copper utensils for birthdays, Christmas, anniversaries; the walls are buckling with hanging sauce pots. We hardly have room in the kitchen work space for the Mr. Coffee between the Cuisinart, the kitchen scales, the twelve-speed blender, the yoghurt maker, the coffee grinder, and a ceramic bowl full of the vast necessary variety of wire whisks and wooden spoons, not to mention the basil, rosemary, tarragon, and thyme potted on the window sills. Our stove has six eyes, two ovens, a broiler, and a griddle, leading agents of Mr. Carter to say that we are a natural gas crisis all by ourselves.

Sometimes, as I race home from the office to get the salad made before starting the Rock Cornish game hens *basquaise,* I look back with momentary nostalgia on a different world of leisurely days, when I scrambled at most a dozen eggs a year and knew nought of the kitchen save how to prize ice trays out of the fridge. Oh, in those days, always a good American, I did singe a steak or two over charcoal every summer and was even known, after infrequently pulling a protesting bass out of friendly waters, to pop the creature, scaled, gutted, and doused in corn meal, into a frying pan full of hot bacon grease. But that was a sometime thing, sport not necessity, a touch of the male animal in the pre-Friedan era when men were men and women roasted the Thanksgiving turkey with oyster stuffing.

Not, I protest, that I have become a cooking freak in middle age out of the pressures of liberation, women's from the galley, men's from macho. Quite the opposite. In a brief period of mid-life bachelorhood, I was addicted to store-bought glazed doughnuts for breakfast and to hitting a different restaurant seven nights a week, carefully spreading the overhead among four different credit cards. *That* was liberation.

But man cannot live by Diners Club alone, and as I undertook new domestic arrangements, a funny thing happened on the way to Sardi's—I discovered that romance blossoms over the kitchen range. There, love thickens like hollandaise, and troths are plighted in the aroma of pot roast in wine. Some couples golf; some travel; others play backgammon. But from the start, Pamela and I baked and broiled.

The reasons are many—a nice sharing of labor, for instance. Say a dinner party for eight or ten. I might undertake a salad and veal scallopini à la Marsala. Pamela will see to the zucchini sautéed in butter, or maybe asparagus vinaigrette, and to cheesecake, of which she is the unchallenged queen (see page 222).

Then there's the neighborhood. On the Upper East Side of New York, the available shops beggar description, from the fishmonger to the greengrocer to the place where you can get fettucine made fresh every morning. They all deliver, too, from telephone orders, which is a convenience few but we New Yorkers can command in this shopping-center wasteland. In the summer, if you know where to go, it's a short hop up to Harlem in the early morning for fresh vegetables trucked in overnight from somewhere around Plains, Georgia. It would be little short of criminal to ignore such abundance in favor of some supercilious maître d' with his palm out.

Do not ignore the aesthetics of the thing. Take a head of Boston lettuce apart, right down to its tiny yellow heart; such intricacies of fit, such repetitions of form, in so many dimensions, no architect or designer could duplicate. And an eggplant gleaming darkly on the butcher block, the rich rising of bread in the oven, a homemade soup bubbling musically in the pot—these among other sensations of the kitchen can only be described as sensuous.

Conviviality is not the least of cooking's attractions. Practically everybody is interested in food, if not in cooking, and few subjects make for more enthusiastic conversation. Sometimes friends gather in our kitchen while the casserole simmers; sometimes others help prepare the feast; but always the kitchen and the table seem to be at the center of things in our house. That's as it should be, in a society where the "family kitchen" remains a cherished tradition, if not often a fact.

Above all, however, cooking is something Pamela and I do together, most of the time. We learn from each other—I more from her, since her cooking is more varied and experienced than mine; but she some things from me, since I'm more experimental. It's something we can share with our children—just recently, I discovered in my Bloomingdale's bills a charge to my son, aged eighteen, for one crepe pan. More power to him. Cooking's a way, too, to maintain tradition; in the bicentennial year, we had an Early American menu for Thanksgiving. Most of Pamela's best recipes came down from her family in Indiana and I've cadged out of my mother the makings of, say, Stonewall Cookbook Brunswick Stew, plus her own secret recipe for what used to be acknowledged at the First Methodist Church of Hamlet, North Carolina, as the best Parker House Rolls in town. Sometime I'll learn how to make *real* North Carolina pork barbecue; we Tarheels don't hold with ketchup.

The kitchen's a place for sharing—secrets, disappointments, frustrations, achievements, surprises, discoveries, one's self with another. Cooking teaches humility—wait till you first try a risotto. It demands respect and generates pride in accomplishment. If you have few standards and no patience for details, better send out for pizza. But for two people working together, with love and diligence, the kitchen is a trysting place.

As to Kathie Wellde, the compiler of this splendid testament to the wide lure of cooking, she's been working on it a long time, not just at typewriter and telephone, not just at the desk where she has somehow coped consecutively with the administrative needs of hapless wretches like me, James Reston, and Bill Safire, but in her Virginia kitchen, testing the goodies, weeding out the culls. Nothing ordinary, she promised me, no Jell-O salads, no frozen specials. The results are not only interesting in origin (see, for example, Dr. Arthur Burns's noninflationary Omelet with Ham, page 157) but challenging in the kitchen (how does the French Embassy's chicken Marengo, page 97, grab you?) and delicious on the table.

But why, you may well ask, another cookbook? Because, goes the short answer, this one's different. So it is, but the longer and better answer is that it's also *like* all *good* cookbooks. It's a work of love, which is what cooking is all about, and why I'm hooked on it, and don't even mind washing the dishes when it comes my turn.

May 4, 1977
New York, N.Y.

GUESS WHO'S IN THE KITCHEN?

Chapter 1

APPETIZERS

KING HUSSEIN

Jordan

His Majesty King Hussein of Jordon makes a state visit to Washington each year. On a recent visit, after he had conferred with the President on their usual subject—the political situation in the Middle East—he met with his ambassador and staff at the Jordanian Embassy.

When the ambassador presented my request for his favorite foods, the King laughed and said that he had received innumerable requests in his lifetime, but never one for a recipe. He ordered the embassy staff to submit instructions for preparing some of his favorite Jordanian dishes: Hummus al Tahini (puréed chick-peas with sesame paste); Baba Ghanouj (puréed roasted eggplant); Tabbouleh (minced spring salad vegetables with cracked wheat); and Maqloobeh (lamb, rice, and eggplant dish).

Arabs, as they are the original "dippers," eat many foods with their hands; utensils are considered unnecessary. Flat round loaves of warm Arab bread are broken into pieces and used to scoop up a bite of the dips—hummus and Baba Ghanouj.

One of the most interesting food customs in Jordan is the *mensef*, (page 46). A mensef is a meal in one huge round dish or tub that is usually prepared for large crowds or family celebrations. However, the literal meaning of mensef is big tray or dish. A whole young lamb is stewed in a mixture of spices and diluted with *laban* (yoghurt). When the meat is tender, rice is cooked in the juice, along with pine nuts, and the mixture is turned out on a huge platter. No plates or utensils are offered; the diners break off a piece of lamb with their fingers, and eat it. Next, a handful of hot rice is scooped up, rolled into a ball in the palm of the hand, and put into the mouth. The guest of honor at the mensef is offered the choicest delicacy—the cooked gray eye of the lamb. It is considered an insult to pass up this morsel, and many Americans strengthen their nerve with whiskey before partaking in this "honor."

BABA GHANOUJ (Eggplant Appetizer)

From King Hussein

1 medium eggplant
⅓ cup tahini (sesame paste)
⅓ cup lemon juice

2 or 3 cloves garlic, mashed
Parsley sprigs

Put whole, unpeeled eggplant in a 350° oven for about 45 minutes until soft when pierced with a fork. When the eggplant has cooled scoop out inside, and purée the scooped-out pulp, tahini, lemon juice, and garlic in a blender. Spread the concoction on a shallow plate or platter and decorate with parsley.

Serve with warm Arab bread. Little chunks of bread are to be torn off the flat loaf and dipped in the Baba Ghanouj.   SERVES 6

AUTHOR'S NOTE: In Jordan the eggplant would be roasted whole over char-coal, and the ingredients mashed together for an hour by hand.

HUMMUS AL TAHINI (Appetizer of Chick-peas)

From King Hussein

2 cups cooked dried chick-peas or
   canned chick-peas, drained
2/3 cup tahini (sesame paste)
3/4 cup lemon juice

2 cloves garlic, mashed
1/2 teaspoon salt
Pure olive oil
Parlsey sprigs

Put chick-peas through a food mill or purée in a blender. It is impossible to purée 2 cups at one time in blender, so do it in 1/2 recipe lots. Slowly add tahini, lemon juice, garlic, and salt. The mixture will be heavy and pasty and it is permissible to put in 1 or 2 teaspoons water to aid the blending (but lie if you do, as no Mid-East gourmet would do this).

When the mixture is smooth, pour or spread onto a platter and pour a little olive oil over the top. Add sprigs of parsley for decoration.

Serve with warm Arab bread (round flat loaves).   SERVES 6

AUTHOR'S NOTE: This is the authentic recipe for hummus, although Jordanians do not have American blenders; I have adapted the recipe to take advantage of this useful gadget.

It is easier to blend about 1/2 the ingredients at one time. If you put all the above in the blender, it will be an unmanageable paste and cause the blender motor to work too hard. Sometimes I remove and discard the skins from the chick-peas (my children call it "chicking them peas"), as it seems to make the blending process easier. Of course if you have a food processor, you can just throw everything in, and a smooth and creamy purée evolves in minutes.

TABBOULEH (Appetizer or Salad)

From King Hussein

1 cup fine burghul or cracked wheat
¾ cup finely chopped onion
½ cup finely chopped scallion,
    including tops
1½ cups chopped fresh parsley
½ cup chopped fresh mint leaves

¼ teaspoon freshly ground black
    pepper
1 teaspoon salt
½ cup lemon juice
¾ cup olive oil
2 or 3 tomatoes, coarsely chopped

Put burghul in bowl and cover with cold water, allowing it to stand about 1 hour. Drain, and with your hands, press out excess water.

Add all other ingredients and mix with the hands.   SERVES 6

AUTHOR'S NOTE: This is a lovely fresh salad, but because of the predominance of mint and the strength of the burghul, it is ideally used for a first course, not as a salad with the dinner.

STEAK TARTARE

From William Safire

3 pounds ground sirloin
1 clove garlic
1 teaspoon capers, plus some juice
1 large red Bermuda onion, diced
Freshly ground black pepper to taste
Salt to taste

1 egg yolk
½ teaspoon dry English mustard
1 tablespoon cut-up anchovies
2 dashes Worcestershire sauce
Oil and wine vinegar to meld

Have the sirloin ground only once.

Squeeze garlic through a garlic press into a large wooden bowl. Add ground meat and all remaining ingredients and mix together well. Press into 4 neat patties and crisscross with a fork for decoration.

Serve on a bed of lettuce with thin pumpernickel or good rye.   SERVES 4

HERINGSCOCKTAIL

From Embassy of Germany

4 salted herring
1 cup milk
1 onion
1 orange
2 dill pickles
1 slice canned pineapple

6 tablespoons tomato ketchup
2 dashes Tabasco sauce
Juice of ½ lemon
2 tablespoons pineapple juice
1 head lettuce
½ cup sour cream

Clean and bone herring and rinse under cold water. Pour milk into pan and soak fillets of herring for 15 minutes.

Cut onion into thin slices. Peel orange and break into sections. Cut pickles, pineapple slice, and orange sections into ½″ slices and toss.

Drain and dry fillets of herring and cut into 1″ strips. Combine with fruit and onion and mix.

Mix ketchup, Tabasco, lemon and pineapple juices. Place in refrigerator for 30 minutes.

Separate lettuce, wash, and toss dry. Lay bed of lettuce leaves in glass dish. Fill with Heringscocktail. Pour ketchup sauce over cocktail and garnish with a dab of sour cream.   SERVES 4

HAM AND CHEESE POKER CHIPS

From Aaron Latham

1 4-ounce package cream cheese
6 Danish ham slices

6 scallions

Spread cream cheese on thin slices of ham. Roll ham and cheese sheets around whole scallions (only tips and ends should be cut off) to form a kind of log with the scallions in the center. Cut across the grain to form disks of ham, cheese, and scallions about the size of poker chips. Serve face up on a platter. If the disks have been cut correctly, they should appear to have tree rings.   SERVES 4

LIVER PÂTÉ NORMANDY (Pâté à la Normande)

From Warren Weaver, Jr.

½ pound (16 tablespoons) butter
½ cup finely chopped onion
2 tablespoons finely chopped shallot
1 cooking apple
1 pound chicken livers
¼ cup calvados or applejack

3 tablespoons cream
1 teaspoon lemon juice
½ teaspoon oregano
1 scant teaspoon salt
¼ teaspoon freshly ground black pepper

Melt 3 tablespoons of the butter in a large heavy skillet, and sauté onion and shallot over moderate heat for 6 minutes, stirring occasionally, until soft and lightly colored. Core, peel, and roughly chop the apple. Add it to the onion mixture and cook for 4 more minutes. Transfer the mixture to the bowl of a food processor.

In the same skillet melt 3 more tablespoons butter. Drain and clean chicken livers, cutting each in half. Sauté over moderate heat for 4 minutes, stirring. Meanwhile, warm the calvados in a small saucepan. When the livers are brown outside but still pink within, take both skillet and saucepan off heat, light apple brandy carefully with a long match, and pour it, flaming, a little at a time into the skillet. Shake the skillet gently from side to side until the flame is out.

Put the metal blade in the processor bowl, and add the onion-apple mixture and the livers with their accumulated liquid. Add cream and process a few seconds until rough-smooth. Put the mixture aside in a bowl to cool.

Return the fully cool mixture to the processor bowl with the metal blade in place. Add the remaining 10 tablespoons chilled butter, thinly sliced, and lemon juice, oregano, salt, and pepper. Process in short bursts until butter bits just disappear—no longer.

Pack the pâté into one or more glass or ceramic containers. Cover with plastic wrap and a lid, if available, and refrigerate for 3–4 hours. (A thin coat of clarified butter on top will provide additional protection against discoloring.)

The pâté may be served in its container or turned out on a plate and decorated with slices of dark olive, pimiento, etc., and garnished with chopped parsley. Don't worry if it refuses to turn out in a neatly molded loaf; it tastes just as good roughly mounded. SERVES 6

GILLESPIE MONTGOMERY

Representative from Mississippi

Gillespie Montgomery is tall and slim, middleaged and dignified. He is chairman of the House Select Committee on Involvement in Southeast Asia and unofficial head of a small Democratic breakfast group which has no name and is mainly social.

He loves to eat southern specialties, including Spoon Bread, Black-eyed Peas with Hog Jowl, Corn Pudding, and Ambrosia, and he has never outgrown peanut butter and jelly. Chicken is also a favorite and should be, as Mississippi is one of the largest poultry farming states.

During a debate by the House Rules Committee on legislation to aid Mississippi's poultry farmers, Congressman Montgomery plunked down a box on the committee table and pulled out a rubber chicken. Committee members laughed and voted to send the bill to the House.

He is also very fond of "finger food" and always makes sure that he has interesting appetizers at his parties. One such appetizer—and an easy one to prepare—is Marinated Mushrooms.

MARINATED MUSHROOMS

From Representative Montgomery

1 pound mushrooms, halved, or 1 10-ounce can mushrooms, drained

1 scant cup Italian-style or herb and garlic salad dressing

Place mushrooms in a container and cover with dressing. Let stand overnight. Drain and serve.

LEMON PEPPER MELBAS

From Representative Montgomery

Spread very soft butter on both sides of very thinly sliced bread. Remove crusts and sprinkle both sides of bread with lemon pepper. Cut into strips and toast in very slow oven until crisp.

AUTHOR'S NOTE: Lemon pepper—dried lemon peel mixed with pepper—is available commercially.

SHRIMPS ORIENTAL (Hors d'Oeuvres)

From Howard Hiatt

1½–2 pounds cooked fresh shrimp
   (large are better)
2 red Bermuda onions, sliced
6 bay leaves
½ pound fresh mushrooms, sliced
1 11-ounce can mandarin oranges
   with juice

¾ cup salad oil
¾ cup white vinegar
2½ teaspoons celery seed
2½ tablespoons capers
Dash Tabasco sauce

Layer shrimp and onions in flat casserole. Add bay leaves, mushrooms, and oranges. Combine remaining ingredients in bowl and pour over shrimp. Cover and refrigerate, to marinate, at least 24 hours.

AUTHOR'S NOTE: Dean Hiatt said this is his sister's recipe. The Hiatts are a cooking family.   SERVES 6

ROBERT McCLORY

Representative from Illinois

Robert McClory is proud of being one of the few members of the House of Representatives who speak French. He went from Illinois public schools to L'Institut Sillig in Vevey, Switzerland, where he later taught (in French) English and elementary subjects. With his fluency in French, his law degree, and his Dartmouth education, he is a valuable member of the Congress. He was chosen United States delegate to the Interparliamentary Union, and he is second-ranking Republican member of the Judiciary Committee.

The congressman is a practiced cook and once appeared on national television gracefully flipping pancakes. He entertains his staff at their Christmas party by making his specialty, Swiss Cheese Fondue, which he learned during his student days in Switzerland. He recalls the romantic Swiss custom of young people around the fondue pot, dipping chunks of bread into the creamy hot cheese. If a girl allows the bread to slip off the fondue fork, the boys in the circle can kiss her. Here is the McClory fondue recipe.

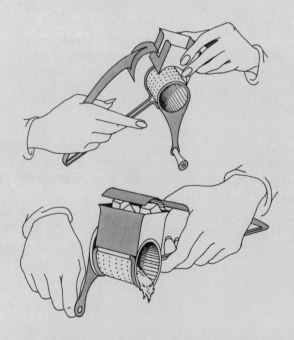

SWISS CHEESE FONDUE

From Representative McClory

1 clove garlic, slightly crushed
2 cups dry white wine (chablis or
* Riesling)*
1 bay leaf
⅔ pound imported Swiss Gruyère
* cheese, grated*

⅓ pound imported Appenzeller
* cheese, grated*
3 tablespoons flour
3 tablespoons kirschwasser
French bread, cut into large cubes

Rub bottom and sides of an earthenware fondue pot or casserole dish (do not use metal) with garlic clove. Add white wine and bay leaf and bring to bubble, but do not boil.

Mix, by tossing lightly with the hand, the cheeses and flour. Spoon in this flour-cheese mixture gradually, stirring all the while with a wooden spoon. The heat should be very low. Continue until the mixture is smooth and creamy. Just before removing the dish from the heat, add kirschwasser. Keep mixture hot over chafing dish or Sterno.

Dip cubes of bread with long-handled fondue forks and eat. If mixture becomes too thick, thin with a little more wine.   SERVES 6

RICHARD SCHWEIKER

Senator from Pennsylvania

Senator Richard Schweiker's checkerboard career included farm work, prize winning debating, and honors at Penn State University, experience in his family's business, and navy duty until he ousted liberal Democrat Joseph Clark from the Senate in 1968.

He is one of the Senate's more liberal Republicans, though he dislikes the label, and his voting record in the sixties and opposition to Supreme Court appointments placed him on Nixon's White House Enemies List.

Richard Schweiker is serious about family (he has five children) and public service and with his long Senate days does not "have enough time to personally get into cooking, but Claire and I have served Shrimp Dip to First Lady Betty Ford, as well as many of my colleagues in the Senate—Senator and Mrs. Frank Church, Senator Mark Hatfield, and the Birch Bayhs."

SHRIMP DIP

From Senator Schweiker

1 8-ounce package cream cheese
¾ cup mayonnaise
1 pound cooked shrimp, diced, or 3
  4½-ounce cans large deveined
  shrimp
1 tablespoon diced onion

1 tablespoon minced celery
1 tablespoon minced green pepper
2 teaspoons lemon juice
¼ teaspoon salt
4 drops Tabasco sauce

Mix all ingredients or blend briefly in blender. Use your favorite crackers or chips for dipping.   SERVES 6

MALCOLM WALLOP

Senator from Wyoming

Senator Malcolm Wallop of Wyoming was born of British parents in New York City. He grew up in Wyoming, where his family had lived for three generations, but came East for his education and graduated from Yale.

The forty-three-year-old freshman Republican owns Polo Ranch, six thousand acres of cattle farm in Big Horn, Wyoming.

Senator Wallop explains that informality and hospitality are the way of life in the West. With miles between ranches, visitors are rare and conversation is treasured. Guests are urged to stay awhile.

Exotic fare is not his specialty, but he cooks everything and finds enjoyment in it. When asked, "Do you ever cook for your Senate colleagues, and do they reciprocate?" he roared and said that he guessed some of them like to cook, "but we sure as hell don't sit around and discuss our recipes."

The directions for Senator Wallop's Boned Venison Sirloin and Wyoming Steak Tartare are pure and authentic Wallop. The flavor of the man and the West are in his words, and cooks will enjoy his colorful instructions.

WYOMING STEAK TARTARE

From Senator Wallop

*3 pounds whole ¾" round steak
  from lean grass-fed beef
¾ cup caraway seeds
1 cup finely chopped peanuts
1 cup finely chopped onion*

*2 hard-boiled eggs, chopped
¾ cup chopped watercress
Anything else you like
1 or 2 cups of your favorite béarnaise
  sauce*

Use silver spoon (hammered from silver bullet). Stainless steel will not work for reasons known only to the beef gods.

Scrape the round steak with silver spoon (do not grind). When finished on one side, flop over. You are left with a pile of pure, lean, unsinewed beef and a pile of pure fat and sinews. Discard latter (Labrador dogs love it); reserve the former. Make into generous ½-pound mounds and chill. Arrange on plates of watercress; arrange various cups of seeds and chopped materials about conveniently. Pour on very hot béarnaise. If you make béarnaise, substitute homemade chokecherry wine vinegar for ordinary (and tasteless) wine vinegar. Change the flavor of each bite by wandering through cups of condiments at random. Prepare for each new flavor with sips of chilled vodka.

Serve with vodka kept in freezer, flavored with lemon peel or caraway seeds— served in shot glasses.

Dish is satisfactory any time of year, anywhere in the country, but is superior on cool Wyoming summer evening after hot day in the hayfield (especially if you don't have to go to the field the next day and can enjoy the vodka in any quantity).   SERVES 6

Chapter 2

SOUPS

JIMMY CARTER

President of the United States

This is a book about the cooking and eating habits of America's prominent men. But the most famous and foremost, President Carter, nearly missed the deadline.

After Jimmy Carter won the election, his staff graciously gathered the Carters' favorite recipes, but months later they were not released for this book. Telephone calls and letters to the White House brought no batch of recipes. They rested on the desk of Press Secretary Jody Powell.

Powell spoke in April at the National Press Club and afterward was given a large, live Georgia frog. The moderator explained that it was to commemorate Jody's classic answer to Lester Maddox during the Carter-Maddox gubernatorial campaign. When Maddox called Carter a liar, Jody shrugged it off with "Being called a liar by Lester is like being called ugly by a frog."

The next day I wrote Jody Powell offering a trade. I would "cook up a mess of frog's legs anytime" in exchange for "my" Carter recipes. The White House sent the recipes promptly.

President Carter prefers to dine simply; for most of his life, eating has been merely a functional necessity. Friends suggest this is navy influence where dinner is "mess call" and just one more detail to be pressed into an already tight schedule. The habit continued during his long campaign for the presidency. A campaign meal was usually a hotel restaurant steak and a glass of milk (not wine) or, as often as not, a sandwich.

Chicken is a favorite with the President (it is often "dressed up" and served at White House dinners), as is eggplant. Rosalynn Carter did the cooking during their Georgia years, except for official dinners at the Governor's Mansion. And occasionally, Jimmy Carter did. During his campaign, he appeared on a TV show doing a "shake and fry," he said, on a fish catch.

Until former peanut farmer James Earl Carter became President of the United States, peanuts, though a familiar part of southern diet, were for many Americans something you bought in a can to serve with cocktails. But the peanut is in fashion now and peanut recipes are being rediscovered. Here is Rosalynn Carter's peanut soup.

PEANUT SOUP

From the home of President Carter

¼ cup finely chopped onion
1 tablespoon butter
½ cup creamy peanut butter
1 10½-ounce can condensed cream
   of chicken soup

2¼ cups milk
¼ cup chopped salted peanuts
Salted peanut pieces
Parsley sprigs
Paprika

Sauté onion in butter until tender but not brown. Mix in peanut butter and cook several minutes longer. Blend in soup and milk. Heat until almost boiling but do not boil. Add the peanuts and stir once or twice.

Serve garnished with additional peanuts, parsley, and paprika. SERVES 4–6

MINESTRONE

From Embassy of Italy

¼ pound dried white beans
2 onions, diced
Olive oil
2 cloves garlic, chopped
5 strips bacon, chopped
1 heaping teaspoon fresh marjoram
   or ½ teaspoon dried
1 heaping teaspoon fresh thyme or
   ½ teaspoon dried
1 heaping teaspoon fresh basil or 1
   teaspoon dried
4 tomatoes or 1 1-pound can
   tomatoes

1½ tablespoons concentrated tomato
   purée
½ cup red wine
6 cups water
2 carrots, diced
1 small turnip, diced
2 small potatoes, peeled and diced
1 stalk celery, diced
Half small cabbage, chopped
½ cup pastina or broken spaghetti
   pieces or small shells or macaroni
4 tablespoons grated Parmesan
   cheese

Soak beans overnight.

Sauté onions in oil. Add garlic, bacon, herbs, tomatoes, tomato purée, and red wine. Let this bubble for a few minutes and add drained beans. Cover all this with water and simmer for 2 hours or until beans are soft. Add carrots, turnip, and potatoes. Cook about 15 minutes and add celery, cabbage, and pasta and cook gently 12–15 minutes.

When you are satisfied that the soup is properly seasoned, add grated Parmesan and serve.

An extra dish of grated cheese should be served with the soup.

AUTHOR'S NOTE: This is excellent. Preparation is time-consuming but can be done in 2 stages (2 days if you like). SERVES 8

FRANK MANKIEWICZ

Political Adviser

Frank Mankiewicz, author, campaign manager for Senator McGovern, adviser to Kennedys, columnist for the Washington *Post,* is an excellent cook. He has been described in the Washington *Post* as "glib, cool, tough." Frank, the cook, is earthy, warm, and relaxed. His New Year's Eve parties have become a Washington tradition and Lentil Soup is his specialty then. The recipe follows.

LENTIL SOUP

From Frank Mankiewicz

1 pound lentils
2 stalks celery, chopped
1 celery root, chopped
2 or 3 leeks, chopped
4 tablespoons chopped onion
3 or 4 tablespoons bacon fat

2 carrots, cut in ½-inch slices
About 4 knackwurst, quartered
Salt and pepper to taste
8 cups water
1 tablespoon flour

Soak lentils overnight.

Put all ingredients but the flour in a pressure cooker (use soaking water as part of the 8 cups). Cook at 15 pounds for 20 minutes. Cook again before serving, just a few minutes this time, with no pressure attachment.

Make a paste of flour and a little water. Add this to give a slight thickening to the soup. SERVES 6

PAUL LAXALT

Senator from Nevada

Paul Laxalt is the Republican senator from Nevada. After graduating from University of Denver Law School and a tour in the U. S. Army, he entered politics as district attorney. He then went from D.A. to lieutenant governor (the only Republican elected official in an otherwise Democratic state) to governor. He was elected to the Senate in 1974.

Senator Laxalt and his family live in Arlington, Virginia. A favorite food is his mother's soup, which he calls Basque Soup.

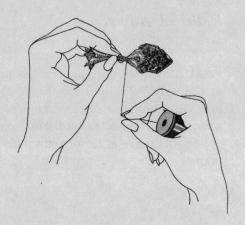

BASQUE SOUP

From Senator Laxalt

6 peppercorns	2 6-ounce cans V-8 juice
1 bay leaf	1½ quarts water
3 sprigs parsley	2 tablespoons salt
6 cloves	2 onions, diced
1 1-inch-long cinnamon stick	4 carrots, diced
3 pounds lean chuck, cut up	3 stalks celery, diced
2 cans chicken broth	2 cups finely chopped cabbage
2 cans beef broth	1 can pimiento, chopped

Make a bouquet garni (tied in cheesecloth) of peppercorns, bay leaf, parsley, cloves, and cinnamon. Cover and simmer chuck, chicken and beef broth, V-8 juice, water, salt, and bouquet garni 1½ hours. Discard bouquet garni. Add onions, carrots, celery, cabbage, and pimiento. Cover and simmer 45 minutes. Serve as thick soup.

Add as a variation ¾ cup pasta; use pastina, stellette, vermicelli broken into inch-long pieces, or any small pasta. SERVES 8

ALAN CRANSTON

Senator from California

Alan MacGregor Cranston had a successful career in his father's Palo Alto real estate firm until 1958 when he became the first liberal Democrat in seventy-two years to win conservative California's office of comptroller of the state. He calls himself a politician "without flamboyance, who is a conservative in fiscal matters, but liberal in human matters." He was elected to the Senate from California in 1967.

TRADER VIC'S BONGO BONGO SOUP

From Senator Cranston

2 tablespoons butter
1 10-ounce jar medium fresh oysters
½ cup water
2 tablespoons chopped spinach
1 quart half-and-half
1 heaping tablespoon cornstarch
mixed with 1 tablespoon water

Dash garlic salt
Dash cayenne pepper
½ teaspoon A.1. sauce
Salt and pepper to taste
Whipped cream, unsweetened, for
topping

Melt butter in saucepan and add oysters, including liquid, plus ½ cup water. Cool slightly, add spinach, and place entire mixture in blender. Blend until smooth.

In the meantime, heat half-and-half to boil. Add oyster and spinach mixture to half-and-half but do not boil. Thicken with cornstarch and water mixture. Add garlic salt, cayenne, and A.1. sauce and appoint with salt and pepper.

To serve, top each individual serving in bowl with 1 heaping tablespoon whipped cream and slip under broiler for a few seconds until cream settles and is golden brown. SERVES 6

WATERCRESS SOUP

From Howard Hiatt

¼ pound butter	1 cup water
2 cups diced onion	2 bunches watercress
1 clove garlic, chopped	2½ cups water
1½ quarts peeled raw potatoes,	2½ cups milk
sliced reasonably thin	⅓ cup dry sherry or white wine
1½ tablespoons salt	(optional)
½ teaspoon freshly ground black	
pepper	

Heat butter in large pot. Add onions and garlic and sauté for 5 minutes. Do not brown. Add potatoes, salt, pepper, and 1 cup water. Cover and cook on low heat until potatoes are tender. Coarsely chop watercress stems and leaves and add to potatoes, stirring in 2½ cups water. Bring to a boil and reduce heat to a simmer for 15 minutes. Cool and purée in a blender.

Before serving, heat and stir in milk. Add dry white wine. Taste this Olympian nectar. SERVES 6

HUBERT HUMPHREY

Former Vice-President of the United States

The late Hubert Horatio Humphrey had an impressive political résumé, having risen to the office of the vice-presidency of the United States under Lyndon Johnson from 1964 to 1968. But the thirty years he spent as a fiery liberal in the United States Senate will mark his place in American history.

Here is his wife Muriel's Beef Soup, which was his favorite.

BEEF SOUP

From the home of Vice-President Humphrey

1½ pounds stew beef or chuck, cut
   up, and soup bone
1 teaspoon salt
½ teaspoon pepper
2 bay leaves
4 or 5 medium carrots, sliced
½ cup chopped onion

1 cup chopped celery
1 cup chopped cabbage
1 No. 2 can Italian-style tomatoes
1 tablespoon Worcestershire sauce
1 beef bouillon cube
Pinch oregano or your preferred
   spice

Cover meat with cold water in heavy 3-quart kettle. Add salt, pepper, and bay leaves. Bring to bubbly stage while preparing vegetables. Turn heat low and add carrots, onion, celery, and cabbage. Simmer at least 2½ hours or until meat is very tender. Remove bone and bay leaves and cut meat into bite-sized pieces. Add tomatoes, Worcestershire, bouillon cube, and oregano. Simmer for ½ hour longer and serve. SERVES 6

BEEF BORSCHT

From the home of Carl Bernstein

3 pounds beef chuck, cut for stew
3 soup bones
2 onions, quartered
6 cups beef broth
2 cups tomato juice
2 1-pound cans julienne beets, with
   juice

Salt and pepper to taste
Juice of 1 lemon
1 tablespoon cider vinegar
2 tablespoons brown sugar
1½ pints sour cream
Chopped dill

Put beef pieces, bones, onions, and beef broth in a large heavy pot. Boil for 15 minutes, skimming off the scum. Add tomato juice, juice from 1 can of beets, salt, pepper, lemon juice, vinegar, and sugar and bring to a boil. Simmer slowly for 2½ hours until beef is tender. Add the beets left over from the juice, the other can of beets, plus juice, heat through, and serve. Put a blob of sour cream (and extra in a side dish) and chopped dill on top of each soup bowl of borscht.

Serve with boiled potatoes and pumpernickel bread. SERVES 6

CONSOMMÉ CELESTINE

From Embassy of Germany

Prepare beef consommé or double consommé.

Make thin pancakes, adding 1 tablespoon minced parsley to the batter. Cut in ¼-inch strips and add to boiling consommé and cook until they are hot. This soup should be full of pancake strips; they are not just a garnish but an ingredient of the soup. Sprinkle soup with chopped parsley.

AUTHOR'S NOTE: Chopped watercress may be substituted for parsley.

SPLIT PEA SOUP (Erbensuppe)

From Embassy of Germany

1½ cups dried split peas
1 medium onion, diced
1 tablespoon bacon fat
1 ham bone (preferably uncooked)
Pinch celery salt or 2 stalks celery
  and a few sprigs parsley

Salt (if necessary)
Freshly ground black pepper
½–¾ cup light cream (optional)

Soak dried peas overnight in 2 cups cold water. In the morning, drain off the water. Measure and add enough more to make 6 cups in all.

Sauté onion until tender in bacon fat in a deep heavy kettle. Add ham bone, peas, seasonings, and the water (6 cups) in which the peas are resting. Cover, bring to a boil, and simmer gently until peas are tender. This will take 1½–2 hours. If you use celery stalks and parsley, remove after cooking for 15 minutes. Stir often, as soup thickens and will burn on bottom of kettle. Remove bone and any fat on surface. Add cream at end of cooking time if you wish.   SERVES 6

PETER RODINO

Representative from New Jersey

Peter Wallace Rodino, Jr., Democrat from New Jersey, has been re-elected to the House of Representatives every term for twenty years. There he serves as chairman of one of the most important committees of the Congress—the Judiciary.

Congressman Rodino is also a man of culture. He writes poems, plays, and has attempted a novel, and he is a theatergoer and opera lover.

Mr. Rodino is discriminating about the food he eats and enjoys fine cuisine, but he wouldn't go into the kitchen and cook. At home, in true Italian fashion, his wife and mother-in-law serve him well.

Marianna Rodino often cooks her husband's favorite—thin veal slices simmered in marsala wine.

ESCAROLE SOUP

From Representative Rodino

2 quarts chicken broth
1 pound escarole, washed and
    chopped
2 tablespoons butter

3 eggs
Salt and pepper to taste
½ cup grated Parmesan cheese

While broth is heating, cook escarole in butter just until tender. Beat eggs with salt and pepper. Add escarole to hot broth, then egg mixture, and mix well. Add cheese and serve.   SERVES 6

AUTHOR'S NOTE: Mrs. Rodino recommends substituting spinach or asparagus for the escarole to make a soup equally delicious. However, spinach or asparagus should be cooked 4 or 5 minutes in the broth before egg is added.

EDWARD I. KOCH

Mayor of New York City

Edward I. Koch (pronounced Kotch) is a New York City bachelor who served as United States congressman for eight years before he was elected mayor of New York in 1977.

The six-foot balding lawyer, a liberal Democrat, enjoyed simple entertaining as a congressman:

"I like to have four or five dinners at my apartment during the year with no more than eight people, where I prepare gazpacho, salad, and steaks, with ice cream for dessert. Since I have no dining room, we all gather around the living room cocktail table. The intimacy makes for an entertaining and sometimes heated conversation."

But now as Gracie Mansion's tenant, Mayor Koch has to bow to more formality.

GAZPACHO

From Mayor Koch

3 ounces olive oil
3 ounces wine vinegar
*Salt and pepper to taste (Crazy
   Jane lemonade pepper if
   available)*
1 quart tomato juice
1 large cucumber, chopped

2 green peppers, chopped
1 6–8-ounce can pimiento, chopped
3 large tomatoes, chopped
3 cloves garlic, diced
*2 large onions (preferably white),
   chopped*

Mix olive oil and vinegar with salt and pepper. Put in a blender, along with remaining ingredients and blend at lowest speed until coarsely ground. Place the contents in the refrigerator for at least 2 hours. The appeal of this gazpacho to me is its thickness and crunchiness.

Serve with croutons. SERVES 8 GENEROUSLY

HOT BORSCHT

From James Vorenberg

1½ pounds stew beef, cut in
 ¾-inch cubes
2 quarts water
4 beef bouillon cubes
2 tablespoons salt
1 teaspoon pepper
1½ cups shredded beets
¾ cup shredded carrots
1 cup shredded turnip
1 large or 2 medium onions,
 chopped

1 stalk celery, chopped
½ cup tomato purée
3 tablespoons white vinegar
1 tablespoon sugar
½ cup sliced beets
¼ cup sliced carrots
1 small or ½ large head cabbage
 (preferably green), shredded

Cut excess fat from beef. Boil gently in pot with capacity of 3½ quarts for 1 hour in water to which bouillon cubes, salt, and pepper have been added.

Add shredded beets, shredded carrots, turnip, onions, celery, tomato purée, vinegar, and sugar to beef pot and simmer 20 minutes. Add sliced beets and sliced carrots to beef pot. Add cabbage and simmer 40 minutes, or until vegetables are tender (other than sliced beets and carrots, which should be somewhat crunchy). Add additional salt and pepper.

Serve with generous portions of sour cream and dark rye bread.   SERVES 8

J. CARTER BROWN

Director of the National Art Gallery

John Carter Brown is director of the National Art Gallery in Washington. He handles this enormous job easily; perhaps he was destined for it. Washington legend has it that when he was twelve, he visited the National Gallery and commented, "I'd like to run that place someday." He got his chance at the age of thirty-four. His interest in art is ingrained, as his parents were art collectors (his father bought a Monet for $100 in Paris in the early 1900s) and founders of museums.

As part of his everyday work, Carter Brown socializes with the well-known and the wealthy. Lucky are the guests who are asked for a small dinner at the Browns' apartment, for Pam Brown is an experienced and excellent cook, and Carter advises and assists in the kitchen. When they entertain, they serve an elegant or unusual soup or other first course, and an equally mouth-watering dessert. The main courses in between must be simple but delicious. Pam thinks many hostesses make a mistake by having every course rich and unusual—the average palate resists such assault. (Her thinking parallels Sir Winston Churchill's own recipe for his famous speeches, which called for a memorable beginning and end.)

Cold Avocado Soup and Meringue Cake (page 230) are the Browns' idea of a memorable beginning and end to a good dinner.

COLD AVOCADO SOUP

From the home of J. Carter Brown

1 avocado	*1 10-ounce can chicken consommé*
1 tablespoon lemon juice	*¾ cup heavy cream, whipped*
Salt and pepper to taste	*Few strips cooked bacon, crumbled*

Mash avocado or put it briefly in a blender. Add lemon juice, salt and pepper, and consommé. Fold in whipped cream and chill. To serve, sprinkle crumbled bacon on top of each cup of soup.   SERVES 4

SOUR AND HOT SOUP

From Senator Nelson

4 dried Chinese mushrooms,
    1–1½ inches in diameter
½ cup canned bamboo shoots
2 3-inch squares fresh Chinese bean
    curd, about ½ inch thick
¼ pound boneless pork
1 quart chicken stock
1 teaspoon salt
1 tablespoon soy sauce

¼ teaspoon freshly ground white
    pepper
2 tablespoons white vinegar
2 tablespoons cornstarch mixed with
    3 tablespoons cold water
1 egg, lightly beaten
2 teaspoons sesame seed oil
1 scallion, including top, finely
    chopped

Prepare ahead: In a small bowl, cover mushrooms with ½ cup warm water and let them soak for 30 minutes. Discard water. With knife or cleaver, cut away and discard tough stems of mushrooms and shred the caps by placing 1 at a time on a chopping board. Cut them horizontally into paper-thin slices and then into thin strips.

Drain the pieces of bamboo shoot and bean curd and rinse them in cold water. Shred them as finely as the mushrooms.

With cleaver or sharp knife, trim the pork of all fat. Then shred it by slicing the meat as thinly as possible and cutting slices into narrow strips about 1½–2 inches long. (AUTHOR'S NOTE: or shred in food processor.)

Have the above ingredients, stock, salt, soy sauce, pepper, vinegar, cornstarch mixture, egg, sesame-seed oil, and scallions within easy reach.

To cook: Combine in a heavy 3-quart saucepan the stock, salt, soy sauce, mushrooms, bamboo shoots, and pork. Bring to a boil over high heat, then immediately reduce heat to low, cover the pan, and simmer for 3 minutes. Drop in bean curd, pepper, and vinegar. Bring to a boil again. Give cornstarch mixture a stir to recombine it and pour it into the soup. Stir for a few seconds until the soup thickens, then slowly pour in beaten egg, stirring gently all the while. Remove the soup from the heat and ladle it into a tureen or serving bowl. Stir in sesame-seed oil, sprinkle the top with scallions, and serve.   SERVES 4

SENATE DINING ROOM

Washington, D.C.

A visitor to Washington usually hopes to meet with his congressman or senator. If he is an important constituent, he may be invited to the Senate Dining Room for lunch, where there is the traditional bean soup, which is plain, but consistently good, and the most well known item on the menu.

The Senate has a continually changing atmosphere—crises occur, foreign dignitaries appear, hubbub reigns—but the Senate Bean Soup remains steady: It is on the menu of the Senate Restaurant every day.

There are several oft-repeated legends on the origins of this culinary tradition.

One story is that Senator Fred Thomas Dubois of Idaho, who served in the Senate from 1901 to 1907, was chairman of the committee that supervised the Senate Restaurant. He gaveled through a resolution requiring that bean soup be on the menu every day.

Another account attributes the bean soup mandate to Senator Knute Nelson of Minnesota, who in 1903 expressed his fondness for it.

In any event, senators and their guests are always assured of a hearty, nourishing dish; they know its delicate flavor can be relied upon.

Not all visitors, however, though they may visit the restaurant, are treated to bean soup. In November 1975 President Anwar Sadat of Egypt came to Washington seeking American good will, American arms, and American aid for his country's ailing economy. He got American hospitality—lunch with congressional leaders in the Senate Restaurant. But no bean soup!

SENATE BEAN SOUP

From Senate Restaurant

2 pounds small Michigan navy
    beans
4 quarts water
1½ pounds smoked ham hocks

1 onion, chopped
Butter for sautéing
Salt and pepper to taste

Wash the beans and soak overnight. Wash and run through hot water until beans are white again. Put beans and ham hocks into 4 quarts hot water and boil slowly approximately 3 hours, covered, stirring occasionally. Braise onion in a little butter and when light brown add to the bean soup. Season with salt and pepper, then serve. Do not add salt until ready to serve (take care with salt, as the ham is salty).   SERVES 10–12

DAVID HALBERSTAM

Journalist

When David Halberstam won a Pulitzer Prize in 1964 for international reporting on the Vietnam War, he had graduated from Harvard and worked for the New York *Times* for seven years. Later he wrote for *Harper's, Esquire, Atlantic Monthly,* and other magazines. He has authored several important books, including *The Best and the Brightest,* and is now writing a book on the rise of the modern media.

During the summer, David prepares leisurely meals at his home on Nantucket Island. After swimming, fishing, or tennis, his friends and house guests gather in the kitchen and everyone helps. In 1976 when Hurricane Belle smashed her way along the Atlantic Coast, he was host to a dozen evacuees, including the family of NBC's John Chancellor, since Halberstam's house was somewhat inland. He enjoyed the role of improvising and feeding the group.

He likes to cook and loves talking about food, and he generously tosses off his recipes. His best dishes are chicken and vegetables in a clay pot, marinated butterfly of lamb, and Ham and Clam Chowder.

HAM AND CLAM CHOWDER

From David Halberstam

6 large chowder clams (or 12
   cherrystones)
1 cup small cubes smoked ham or
   pork butt, uncooked
3 medium leeks, diced
2 medium onions, diced

2 stalks celery, diced
4 tablespoons butter
4 large potatoes, peeled and diced
Salt and pepper to taste
1 pint cream

Clean and open clams according to your usual method.* Reserve the juice.
(Cookbook author Joseph Hyde, who taught Halberstam to make this chowder,
says put a bowl under the clams as you open and put a bowl under your elbows,
as well.) Chop the clams. Sauté leeks, onions, and celery in butter until wilted.
Add potatoes, salt and pepper, and water to cover. Simmer until potatoes are
cooked but not mushy. The water should be somewhat evaporated. Heat cream
in a separate pan. Add clams and juice to vegetables, cook 1 or 2 minutes, add
hot cream, and serve. SERVES 4

* See page 123 for opening and cleaning instructions, according to Joe Hyde and Craig
Claiborne.

Chapter 3

ENTREES

MEAT

JOHN TOWER

Senator from Texas

John Goodwin Tower is a genial, outgoing man, conservative of dress and politics. Before politics, he was in the Navy, then became an insurance agent and a radio announcer. He won a special election to the Senate in 1961 to fill the seat vacated by Lyndon Johnson. This won him the distinction of being the first Republican senator from Texas in nearly one hundred years.

Senator Tower is also a cook and performs enthusiastically in Washington's Chili Cook-off each year. Prominent "tasters" judge the chili and recently the judges were their black-tie Excellencies, the ambassadors from Iran, Germany and Great Britain. They joked about the difficulties of discrediting one senator's dish while awarding another's. "Awkward diplomacy," said one; "none of us wants to have trouble with the Hill."

Recently Senators Tower and Goldwater insulted each other, albeit in a friendly manner. When Tower's chili (no beans) won the cook-off, Senator Tower noted Goldwater in third place and announced that the Arizona Senator had "done worse than he did in sixty-four."

Here is Senator Tower's prize-winning chili.

CHILI

From Senator Tower

3 pounds beef or game, cut into
    cubes
1 15-ounce can tomato sauce
1 cup water
1 teaspoon Tabasco sauce
3 heaping tablespoons chili powder
    of ground chili peppers
1 heaping tablespoon oregano
1 heaping teaspoon cumin (comino)
    powder

2 onions, chopped
Garlic to taste
1 teaspoon salt
1 teaspoon cayenne powder
1 level teaspoon paprika
12 small, hot red peppers
4 or 5 chili pods
2 heaping tablespoons flour

Sear meat until gray. Add tomato sauce and water. Add all remaining ingredients except flour and simmer for 1 hour 15 minutes.

Mix flour with enough water to make a paste and stir into chili. Simmer additional 30 minutes.   SERVES 6

BERNDT VON STADEN

Ambassador from West Germany

Mit den besten Empfehlungen der Botschaft der Bundesrepublik Deutschland

With the compliments of the Embassy of the Federal Republic of Germany

His Excellency Berndt von Staden is an American's version of a typical European diplomat. He is correct, polished, highly intelligent, and sophisticated, wears a fine ambassadorial suit—navy blue pinstripe with a white shirt, a discreet tie—he is immaculate and "pressed down." His face has a pronounced squint, perhaps from holding a monocle in place for years.

Baroness Wendelgard von Staden had her own career as a diplomat. She completed a tour in Washington, D.C., in 1961.

The Von Stadens always worry about the battle of the waistline. They like to eat, but in such a social job, they are constantly offered food and drink.

The Von Stadens pointed out that climate influences cooking everywhere and that German food is traditionally heavy since the temperature is cold or cool year round in Germany. If they attempt to serve a traditional German menu for embassy entertaining, they plan it for fall or winter. A typical offering is:

> Fillets of Herring
> Consommé Celestine
> Saddle of Venison
> Spätzle with Lingenberries
> Red Cabbage
> Cucumber Salad
> Götterfreude (Friend of the Gods)

SADDLE OF VENISON

From Embassy of Germany

Saddle of venison should be marinated either in sour milk or in juice of 1 lemon and ½ cup olive oil for at least 3 hours.

Crush 1 teaspoon juniper berries with 1 teaspoon salt and rub into meat. Lay venison, larded side down, in a roasting pan, add 1 onion separated into rings, a 3-inch curl of lemon peel, and ½ cup vinegar. Pour ½ cup simmering melted butter over the meat. Roast for 15 minutes in a moderate oven (350°). Pour over it 1 cup hot sour cream and roast for 45 minutes more, basting frequently. Add 1 more cup hot sour cream during roasting. Turn venison and continue to roast. Allow 20 minutes per pound for medium rare. A pinch of curry powder can be added toward the end.

Garnish with boiled apples and lingenberries: Peel 4 medium apples, cut in half, and core. Boil in water with vinegar until tender but so that they do not lose shape after removing. Let cool. Fill with lingenberries (*Preiselbeeren*) and heat again in oven. SERVES 6

SWISS VEAL RAGOUT

From Embassy of Switzerland

Salt and pepper	*4 tablespoons butter, clarified*
1 pound tender white veal, cut in small pieces	*¾ pound champignons (mushrooms), washed and sliced*
½ cup flour	*2 cups cream*

Salt and pepper meat, powder with flour, and brown slightly in butter.

Sauté the champignons for a few minutes in a little butter. Heat cream and add to champignons and veal, adding more seasonings if necessary. Simmer all together, but do not boil, as meat will get tough, for 20 minutes or until meat is tender.

Veal ragout is usually served with Pan-fried Potatoes (Roesti) (page 146). SERVES 4

AUTHOR'S NOTE: Switzerland is a dairy-rich country and I think this recipe reflects overuse of dairy products. Therefore I suggest half milk and half cream in place of cream.

MEAT SAUCE FOR SPAGHETTI

From Senator Griffin

1 pound lean ground beef	2 cloves garlic, chopped
2 tablespoons olive oil	1 tablespoon chopped green pepper
½ cup minced onions	1 tablespoon salt
2 6-ounce cans tomato paste	¼ teaspoon pepper
2 1-pound cans tomatoes	1 tablespoon Worcestershire sauce
½ pound fresh mushrooms, halved	1 teaspoon sugar
½ stalk celery, chopped	½ teaspoon allspice

Brown meat in oil. Add other ingredients and simmer slowly for several hours. Add water as needed.   SERVES 6–8

AUTHOR'S NOTE: Many people cook spaghetti sauce for several hours, but to me this seems unnecessary. I cook Senator Griffin's sauce for no longer than 1 hour.

JOHN GLENN

Senator from Ohio

John Glenn, Jr., won national fame as the first American to orbit the earth in a space capsule. Before that he served with the Marines in World War II and was a military test pilot in Korea. He was awarded the Distinguished Flying Cross five times. He has enjoyed several successful business enterprises and in 1970 ran unsuccessfully for a Senate seat in Ohio, which he captured four years later. He has also hosted an NBC-TV historical documentary program.

John married his childhood sweetheart, Annie, and they have two children. Annie's Ham Loaf is one of the senator's favorite dishes.

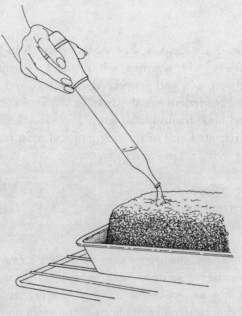

HAM LOAF

From Senator Glenn

1 pound cured ham, ground
½ pound fresh ham, ground
1½ cups dry bread crumbs
2 eggs
¾ cup milk
Pepper to taste

DRESSING GLAZE:
½ cup water
¼ cup vinegar
¼ cup sugar
1 tablespoon dry mustard

Mix both hams, bread crumbs, eggs, milk, and pepper well and form into a loaf. Mix dressing ingredients and pour over loaf. Bake at 350° for 1½ hours, basting frequently.   SERVES 6

BEEF BIRDS WITH SAUCE
(Paupiette de Coeur de Boeuf avec la Sauce)

From Senate Restaurant

1 small onion, chopped
⅛ clove garlic, crushed
8 ounces fresh spinach, chopped
2 tablespoons butter
1 pound ground chuck
¼ cup white cream sauce

1 teaspoon dried parsley
Sherry to taste
Oregano to taste
Salt and pepper to taste
4 pounds beef tenderloin

Sauté onion, garlic, and freshly washed spinach in butter. Add ground beef and brown. Slowly add warmed white sauce, stirring constantly. Add parsley, sherry, oregano, salt, and pepper. Allow to cool and thicken.

Slice raw tenderloin on the bias (45°) in ¼-inch slices. Roll a portion of ground beef mixture inside of each slice and hold together with a toothpick. Place on preheated grill or roasting pan and roast for 10 minutes at 425°.

SAUCE:

2 shallots, chopped	1 cup beef consommé
8–10 fresh mushroom caps	½ teaspoon cornstarch
3 tablespoons butter	1 ounce red wine

Sauté shallots and mushroom caps in butter. Remove mushrooms and set aside. Add consommé to sautéed shallots. Stir until warm. Dissolve cornstarch in water and add to consommé mixture, stirring until thickened. Add red wine. Place mushroom cap on each plate of tenderloin and add sauce as desired.

SERVES 8

BARRY GOLDWATER

Senator from Arizona

Elder statesman Barry Goldwater was a New Year's Day baby in 1909, an elected United States senator, riding to power on General Eisenhower's coattails (by his own admission) in 1952, and a popular, if unsuccessful, presidential candidate in 1964.

He likes chili and beans and Mexican foods. Each year he takes part in the Congressional Chili Cook-off at the National Press Club in Washington and enjoys the rivalry over the merits of Arizona versus Texas chili. Senator Tower's comments and recipe are on page 37.

If you happen to have a few jars of pickled black walnuts, you can enjoy the Goldwaters' favorite supper dish. The senator's mother made the original Black Walnut Stew.

BLACK WALNUT STEW

From Senator Goldwater

2 cups beef broth

6 pounds chuck, cubed, and some rib bones

1 large onion, halved

1 pound ground round, ground twice

3 pint jars pickled black walnuts

Flour for thickening (preferably brown or wheat)

Salt and pepper to taste

Pour broth over chuck, rib bones, and onion and add enough water to cover. Cook slowly about 4 hours, until tender. Skim off fat and remove bones.

Make ground round into small meatballs and add to broth. Cook about 40 minutes.

Mash 1 jar walnuts and add, with juice, to stew. Cook for another ½ hour.

Thicken with flour and add the 2 remaining jars of walnuts and salt and pepper to taste.

Serve over rice or noodles.   SERVES 8–10

DAN SCHORR

Author, TV Commentator

Dan Schorr, former television commentator for CBS and now a syndicated newspaper columnist, is author of *Clearing the Air*, an account of his role in the Pike Report controversy which led to his resignation from CBS.

He says that he is not a cook and that he proposed to his wife, Lee, while eating his favorite food, Liver and Onions, that she prepared.

Lee Schorr adds: "I almost lost him when I cooked for the first time and prepared it the German way with apples. I now simply prepare liver and onions but take great care not to overcook or undercook the liver."

This is, of course, the secret of good liver and onions.

LIVER AND ONIONS

From Dan Schorr

1 large onion, thinly sliced
*2 or 3 tablespoons butter or bacon
  drippings*

1 pound calf liver, sliced
Flour (optional)
Salt and pepper to taste

This is a quick process. The liver should not be overcooked: just 2 or 3 minutes on each side.

Sauté onion in butter or bacon fat. Set aside and keep warm.

Dredge liver slices in flour and fry in butter or bacon fat 2 or 3 minutes on each side. Salt and pepper to taste.

To serve, arrange each slice of liver with onions spooned on top.   SERVES 2

GRILLED KIDNEYS AND SWEETBREADS

From William Rice

2½ pounds veal sweetbreads
1 tablespoon lemon juice or vinegar
1 bay leaf (optional)
*2 tablespoons chopped fresh basil or
  2 teaspoons dried*
10–12 peppercorns, crushed
1 tablespoon chopped fresh parsley
1 teaspoon salt
2 tablespoons wine vinegar

1 tablespoon brandy
*1 cup (approximately) oil (a
  mixture of olive and salad to
  taste)*
2 dozen fresh mushroom caps
2 pounds lamb kidneys
*1 tablespoon fresh thyme or 1
  teaspoon dried*
Salt and pepper to taste

The night before or the morning of the meal, prepare sweetbreads. Place them in cold water and soak, changing water once or twice, for 30 minutes. Drain. Transfer sweetbreads to a large saucepan, cover with water, add lemon juice and bay leaf, and bring to simmer. Cook for 12–15 minutes. Drain and place on platter or in baking dish in a single layer. Cover and refrigerate.

Combine basil, peppercorns, parsley, salt, vinegar, brandy, and ¾ cup oil in a bowl. Toss mushroom caps in this mixture. Cover and marinate for at least 1 hour. If preparing mushrooms in morning, store in refrigerator.

Split kidneys in half and cut away knobs of fat. A half hour before cooking, lift mushrooms from marinade. Replace them with sweetbreads. Toss. Rub kidneys lightly with unused oil and sprinkle with thyme. Thread kidneys and sweetbreads on separate skewers, apportioning mushroom caps among both.

In an oven broiler or over coals, cook sweetbread skewers for 5–7 minutes. Turn, baste with marinade, and place kidney skewers under or over heat. Turn kidneys and baste with oil after 3 minutes or when drops of blood appear on surface. Cook all for another 3 or 4 minutes (kidneys should remain rare within).

Empty skewers onto serving platter, season with salt and pepper, and pour over pan juices if cooked in oven. Serve at once.   SERVES 6

MAQLOOBEH (Arab Upside-down Casserole)

From King Hussein

1 large eggplant, cut in ½-inch slices	*1 large onion, sliced*
	1–2 cups water
½ cup olive or salad oil	*1 cup pine nuts*
1½ pounds cubed lamb	*Rice (see below for quantity)*

If time permits, soak eggplant in cold heavily salted water for 1 hour, drain and dry. (By soaking, the eggplant will absorb less oil as you fry it.) Fry slices in olive or salad oil and set aside.

Fry lamb pieces, then add onions, and when nicely browned, add water and simmer until meat is tender. Drain off broth and reserve. Fry pine nuts a little.

Measure rice and broth from meat, using the proportions 1 cup rice to 1¼ cups broth. Arrange meat in a large, heavy, deep pot. Put layer of pine nuts, eggplant, then rice. Repeat layers if you wish. Cover pot and cook about 25 minutes, until rice is done.

Remove cover and place tray or large plate over pot; slowly turn pot over onto plate. Leave the pot standing like this so all will fall out and hopefully form into a graceful mold.

Serve with yoghurt as side dish.   SERVES 6

AUTHOR'S NOTE: This recipe did not come from Jordan's embassy, but it is authentic and is so delicious that it deserves space.

Maqloobeh can also be made with cauliflower or broad beans instead of eggplant. Also delicious made with beef instead of lamb.

MENSEF (Jordanian Lamb and Rice)

From Embassy of Jordan

1 large lamb (see note)
Salt and pepper to taste
Allspice to taste
Cardamon to taste
4 pounds jameed (see note)

8 ounces ghee (clarified butter)
8 pounds rice
Pine nuts
10 or 12 loaves round Arabic bread

Cook lamb in pieces in a small quantity of water and spices until half done. Add jameed and simmer until lamb is tender. Add ghee, reserving some for pine nuts. In another pot, cook rice. Sauté pine nuts in ghee.

Open loaves of Arabic bread and spread them on a tray or platter, leaving an edging of bread around the rim. Spread some of the sauce in which the lamb cooked over bread, pile rice into high mound on bread, and ladle more sauce over that. Arrange pieces of meat around rice, crowning it with head of the lamb. Sprinkle sautéed pine nuts generously over the whole dish.

Serve with an extra bowl of sauce.

Custom demands that you use the right hand to scoop up both rice and meat, form it into a small ball, and with a flick of the thumb, toss it into the mouth.

SERVES 20

AUTHOR'S NOTE: The age of the lamb should be at least 5 months for proper flavor and not over a year for proper tenderness.

Jameed is preserved, sun-dried, reconstituted yoghurt. Fresh yoghurt cooked with flour or cornstarch to keep it from separating is a workable substitute.

VEAL WITH TUNA SAUCE (Vitello Tonnato)

From Clifton Daniel

Roast veal (leftover veal is fine)
1 3½-ounce can good white tuna fish, with oil
1 tablespoon light cream
3 tablespoons white cider vinegar

¼ cup pure olive oil
3 or 4 capers
2 (or more) anchovies, well drained
1 medium clove garlic, sliced

Slice cold roast veal thinly (good white plume de veau should be chosen from the market, if possible) and arrange slices on a platter.

Blend in a blender tuna (with its oil), cream, vinegar, olive oil, capers, 2 anchovies, and garlic. When the sauce is creamy but not runny, pour over the slices of veal, decorate with more anchovies if you wish, and serve. If the sauce is too thick, add additional oil and cream in last minute of blending. SERVES 4–6

ROBERT PACKWOOD

Senator from Oregon

Senator Robert Packwood came from the Oregon state legislature to his Senate seat in 1968, defeating Wayne Morse, who had represented Oregon for nearly a quarter of a century.

He credits Oregon's other Republican senator, Mark Hatfield, with influencing him to pursue a career in politics when Packwood was a political science student of Hatfield's at Willamette University.

The only time Senator Packwood operates in the kitchen is to open a can of soup when no one else is home or to make marinade for flank steak. When the charcoal flames grow too intense during the barbecuing, the senator diminishes them with his children's squirt guns. Here is his flank steak recipe.

MARINATED FLANK STEAK

From Senator Packwood

½ cup soy sauce
½ cup red wine
1 cup water

2-pound piece of flank steak
¾ teaspoon ground ginger
Good pinch garlic powder

Combine soy sauce, wine, and water, place flank steak in marinade, and sprinkle ginger and garlic liberally over meat. Allow to stand for 4–24 hours. Cut meat in 2-inch strips and barbecue, taking care not to further salt it—the marinade is salty.　　　　　　　　　　　　　　　　　　　　　　　　　SERVES 4

MEAT　　　　　　　　　　　　　　　　　　　　　　　　　　　　　　　**47**

ART BUCHWALD

Syndicated Columnist

Art Buchwald began his career as a columnist in 1949 when he convinced the editors of the Paris Edition of the New York *Herald Tribune* that he should exploit humor with "Art Buchwald in Paris." He did this for a dozen years. In 1962 he abandoned his Paris column and returned to Washington against the advice of his friends. But now his Washington *Post* column, "Capitol Punishment," is an American institution.

When Art is not entertaining at the Sans Souci Restaurant (his private table is ready and reserved at all times), he enjoys Parsley and Lamb Stew, prepared by his wife, Ann, herself an author and successful Washington literary agent. She adds, "If Art is on a diet (usually), I leave out the beans. If he looks slim and trim, I add them."

LAMB AND PARSLEY STEW

From Art Buchwald

6 tablespoons butter
4 large bunches parsley, chopped
16 scallions, chopped (including tops)
3 pounds lean lamb, cubed
Salt and freshly ground black pepper to taste
Juice of 2 lemons

1 lemon, quartered
Chicken broth to cover
5 cups white beans, cooked according to package directions (canned kidney beans may be substituted but are not nearly so good)

In a heavy pot heat 4 tablespoons of the butter, add parsley and scallions, and cook until parsley turns dark green.

In a large skillet or casserole heat remaining 2 tablespoons butter, add meat, and brown lightly. Don't add meat all at once or it fails to brown and just simmers in its juice. Season with salt and pepper. Add meat to vegetable mixture, scraping the skillet to include nice brown scraps. Add chicken broth to cover meat. Add lemon juice and lemon. Cover and simmer until meat is almost tender, about 1–1½ hours. Add beans and correct seasoning. Continue cooking until meat is tender. SERVES 6–8

AUTHOR'S NOTE: This is one recipe I have prepared often. It is unfailingly delicious. However, I omit lemon wedges, as they are unpleasant to bite into and seemed to make the dish just too lemon-sour. Also, I suggest 3 cups cooked white beans instead of 5.

ANTAL DORATI

Director of the Detroit Symphony

Antal Dorati was the music director of the National Symphony Orchestra in Washington from 1970 to 1977, when he left to become director of the Detroit Symphony. When he is not practicing or conducting music, he is the center of attraction at social gatherings to benefit his orchestra.

When the Doratis are not in Washington or Detroit, they occupy their villa in St. Adrian, Switzerland, near Lucerne. The maestro's second wife is an Austrian, Ilse von Alpenheim, a young, attractive concert pianist. When she is in Europe giving a concert tour, Dorati has to "batch" it for a few weeks. "Ilse left an egg in the refrigerator for me and told me how to boil it, but I couldn't."

The Maestro loves to eat—"I enjoy it tremendously, but I have never cooked for myself. If I did it would be just meat and main dishes."

Here is a recipe for Hungarian Goulash, one of his favorite dishes.

Washington decorator Susanne Shaw, a Hungarian baroness and long-time friend of Antal Dorati (and of mine), often prepares the gulyas below for him.

HUNGARIAN GOULASH
(Szekely Gulyas, sometimes called Kaposta Gulyas)

From Antal Dorați

1 onion, coarsely chopped	*1 pound beef, cubed*
3 tablespoons bacon fat	*1 ham hock or smoked pork knuckle*
1 heaping tablespoon paprika (see	*½ cup dry red wine*
note)	*2 cups sauerkraut*
1 pound pork, cubed	*1½ cups sour cream*

Sauté onion in bacon fat only until soft; stir in paprika. Watch carefully, as paprika burns easily, and stir and cook 2 or 3 minutes longer. Put in chunks of pork and beef and stir over heat 10 minutes, until the meat loses its raw color. Put in ham hock or smoked pork and wine and simmer until meat chunks are tender, perhaps 1–1½ hours.

Drain sauerkraut. It is best to use "fresh" sauerkraut which is usually kept in its brine in heavy plastic bags at the grocer's or in barrels at some meat markets and delicatessens. Canned sauerkraut is second choice. Run the sauerkraut, draining in strainer, under cold water for 1 minute. Mix sauerkraut into meat mixture and cook about 1 hour, using simmer heat. Just before serving stir sour cream into the Gulyas and serve. SERVES 6

AUTHOR'S NOTE: You should use good sweet Hungarian paprika; if you must use ordinary American paprika, use much less, as it is strong and biting.

STUART SYMINGTON

Senator from Missouri

Before winning a Senate seat from the state of Missouri, Stuart Symington was an army officer, a businessman, an assistant secretary of war for air under Truman, and First Secretary of the Air Force.

Senator Symington's hawk-to-dove posture typifies the change in America's history in recent decades. He came to national prominence as First Secretary of the Air Force, an advocate of massive military power; and he closed his public career by warning of the dangers of a world-wide arms race.

The senator is not a cook, but a well-traveled "eater" and he took the time to collect a recipe for Bul Go Gi when he was in Korea recently. "It is really tasty," he said.

BUL GO GI (Savory Beef)

From Senator Symington

The savory beef that is frequently prepared at the Commander U. S. Forces Korea Mess is a popular Korean native dish called Bul Go Gi. The tasty bite-sized slices of thin beef are marinated to delight a gourmet's taste the world over.

2 pounds beef tenderloin, thinly
   sliced
2 large scallions, thinly sliced
1 clove garlic, minced
1 tablespoon brown sugar
½ cup soy sauce
1 tablespoon sesame seed

3 tablespoons salad oil
½ teaspoon salt
¼ teaspoon black pepper
½ teaspoon MSG
⅛ teaspoon dried crushed red
   pepper (optional)

Mix all ingredients together and marinate for approximately 2 hours. Arrange meat on broiler rack. Spoon a little marinade on meat and broil meat to desired doneness, perhaps 1 minute on each side. Pour meat drippings from broiler pan over cooked meat and serve.   SERVES 6

MINCE (Hamburger Gravy)

From James Reston

1 pound ground chuck	Salt and pepper to taste
1 medium onion, chopped	1 beef bouillon cube
1 small green pepper, chopped	Flour for thickening
(optional)	Mashed potatoes

Cook meat loosely. Add onion and green pepper and continue to cook. Remove some of the fat which has accumulated in the pan, season with salt and pepper, add about 2 cups water and bouillon cube, and cook 15 minutes. Add water to flour to make a paste and stir into meat mixture to thicken slightly.

Pour the mixture into a pie pan and spread mashed potatoes (instant mashed can be used) over the top. Bake in a preheated 350° oven for about 20 minutes.

SERVES 4

COUNTRY HAM

From Senator Brock

Method for cooking a Tennessee country ham, preferably, or one from Virginia, such as Smithfield:

Cover ham with cold water, after trimming somewhat, and soak for 24 hours. Discard water.

Put in roaster with 7 cups cold water, or as a variation, use half water and half maple syrup. We use the latter.

Put ham and liquid in a preheated 500° oven for 15 minutes. Turn heat off and allow ham to stay in the warm oven for 3 hours. Do not open oven door. Then cook ham again 15 minutes at 500°. Turn heat off and leave ham in warm oven for another 3 hours. It is all right to leave the ham in the oven overnight.

Next, make a glaze:

⅔ cup brown sugar	½ cup hot water
1 teaspoon mustard	

Glaze the ham and bake at 325° for 20 or 30 minutes.

DAVID EISENHOWER

Lawyer, Author

Dwight David Eisenhower II, grandson of a president and husband of a president's daughter, has spent most of his twenty-eight years in school. He is a graduate of Amherst College and George Washington University's law school. He has written for publication, including articles in the New York *Times*. He has recently practiced law in New York City, and is now working on a biography of President Eisenhower.

David cooks occasionally, is an enthusiastic eater, and will try anything new. He pan-fries a great steak and his favorite dishes are Cheese Grits and Hot Fruit Salad.

PAN-FRIED STEAK

From David Eisenhower

Season sirloin or any kind of good steak with any popular pepper seasoning (as Lawry's). Put a piece of butter and the steak in a heavy black skillet. Have heat high for a couple of minutes, then reduce it to medium. Cook steak 3 or 4 minutes on each side, depending on thickness.

The initial extreme heat causes a bit of burning and gives a nice charcoal flavor. Pan-frying also has the advantage over broiling of the steak swimming around in its own juices, rather than losing them to the coals.

AUTHOR'S NOTE: There are two kinds of steak cooks. The ones who broil only and look down on pan-frying; and the black-skillet chefs who consider broiling newfangled. David and I are old-fashioned.

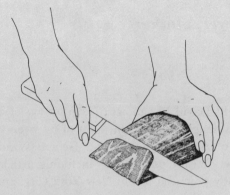

MEAT AND SPINACH LOAF

From Craig Claiborne*

1 pound loose fresh spinach or 1 10-ounce package frozen
1¼ pounds ground veal, pork and beef combination
½ cup fresh bread crumbs
Salt to taste
1½ teaspoons freshly ground black pepper
¼ teaspoon grated nutmeg

½ cup coarsely chopped celery
½ cup loosely packed parsley, chopped
¼ cup milk
½ clove garlic, finely minced
1 tablespoon butter
½ cup finely chopped onion
2 eggs, lightly beaten
3 slices bacon

If the spinach is in bulk, pick it over to remove any tough stems. Rinse the spinach well in cold water, drain, place in saucepan, and cover. It is not necessary to add liquid. Cook about 2 minutes, stirring once or twice. Transfer to colander. Drain and press with hands to extract most of moisture. Chop the spinach.

Put meat in a mixing bowl and add the chopped spinach. Add bread crumbs, salt, pepper, and nutmeg.

Put celery, parsley, and milk in the container of an electric blender. Blend well and add to meat mixture. Add garlic.

Heat butter in a skillet and add onion. Cook until wilted and add to meat mixture. Add eggs and blend well with hands. Shape and fit into an oval or round baking dish or place in loaf pan. Cover with bacon and bake in a preheated 350° oven for 1¼–1½ hours.

Pour off fat and let loaf stand for 20 minutes before slicing.   SERVES 6–8

* From *Craig Claiborne's Favorites from the New York Times,* by Craig Claiborne.

VEAL PICCATA

From Arthur Burns

6 or 8 lean fillets of veal, very thinly sliced and beaten flat	Butter
	2 tablespoons marsala
Flour for dusting	2 tablespoons chicken or meat stock

Dust veal pieces with flour. Fry quickly in sizzling butter in heavy frying pan. add marsala and stock. Stir well. Reduce heat and cook about five minutes.

Serve with mushrooms and rice.   SERVES 2

WILLIAM MACOMBER

President of the Metropolitan Museum of Art

William Macomber ended his government career in 1977 after spending the last five years in the "one more Ambassadorial post on the Firing Line" he always wanted. Bill, who has degrees from Harvard, Yale, and the University of Chicago, spent twenty years in government service with positions in the CIA and several in the State Department. He was special assistant to Secretary of State John Foster Dulles, deputy undersecretary of state, and ambassador to Jordan before his final post as ambassador to Turkey. He has recently been appointed president of the Metropolitan Museum of Art.

Bill, who married Phyllis Bernau in 1963, was a bachelor when President Kennedy appointed him ambassador to Jordan in 1961. His idea of a gourmet meal then was a hamburger (as American as could be put together in the Mideast, which meant a native cook first set yeast dough into facsimile hamburger rolls) accompanied by a simulated milk shake, made with powdered milk, as the local milk is goat's milk. When he didn't serve hamburgers and shakes, Bill would prepare another specialty—a can of corned beef hash, mixed with a can of chili con carne—for a few friends who might come to his official residence after a formal reception.

Had we used the word "chauvinist" in those days, it would have described Bill Macomber. He is very masculine, forceful, and extremely popular, but completely unskilled in domestic science. His wife, Phyllis, former personal secretary to Secretaries of State John Foster Dulles and Dean Rusk, has come a long way in domesticating her husband. He now cooks, unassisted, and his favorite dish to prepare is Shepherd's Pie.

SHEPHERD'S PIE

From William Macomber

5 cups (approximately 2½ pounds) ground round
1 cup chopped onion
¼ cup Worcestershire sauce
3 beef bouillon cubes dissolved in 2 cups water
3 heaping teaspoons cornstarch
Tomato ketchup
10 medium-plus size potatoes (approximately 4 pounds), boiled till soft and peeled

1 cup milk
4 tablespoons butter
Salt and pepper to taste
2 egg yolks
1 tablespoon milk
Paprika

Mix ground meat with onion and brown 10–15 minutes. Mix in Worcestershire sauce.

Heat bouillon and add cornstarch to thicken. Slowly add the bouillon mixture to the ground steak and onion mixture. Put meat mixture in 3-quart 13″×8″ Pyrex casserole dish. The meat should fill up the bottom half of the dish. Spread a thin layer of ketchup across the top surface of the meat.

Mash potatoes with 1 cup milk and the butter. Add salt and pepper and spread the mixture evenly over the meat mixture so that it resembles a very thick pie crust. The layer of mashed potatoes should be about as thick as the layer of meat below it.

MEAT

With a fork, beat egg yolks and 1 tablespoon milk. Having cleaned the top of the rim of the casserole, spread the egg-milk mixture over the potatoes. Then put an even, light sprinkling of paprika all over the top. Bake in a preheated 350° oven for about 25 minutes (when the meat can be seen bubbling through the casserole glass) and serve.   SERVES 8

AUTHOR'S NOTE: A fluted edge of mashed potatoes makes the dish more attractive to serve.

ZURICH COUNCILLOR DISH
(Zurcher Ratsherrentopf)

From Embassy of Switzerland

Shallots
Oil
1 ¼ carrots, sliced
2 cups green peas
Salt and pepper to taste
4 or 5 potatoes
Several small slices of meat, such as
    pork, veal, and beef steaks

Several slices of kidney, liver, or
    brain (or all three)
Bacon and several small veal or pork
    sausages
Butter

Sauté shallots in a little oil, add sliced carrots and peas, season with salt and pepper, and stew until tender, adding a little water.

Peel potatoes, cut in cubes or globules, and fry in butter or oil until soft.

Fry or grill the different slices of meat and season; fry bacon and sausages slightly.

Arrange the vegetables and fried potatoes on a plate or in an earthenware pot. On top of it, display the slices of meat. Add a piece of butter and let it melt.   SERVES 4

MIKE MANSFIELD

Senator from Montana

Senator Mike Mansfield of Montana has come full circle in his political career. He was chosen by President Roosevelt in 1944 as his personal envoy to China. After thirty-four years as congressman and majority leader of the Senate, and five presidents later, he was named by President Carter in 1977 as ambassador to the People's Republic of China.

Mike Mansfield remembers long days in the Butte mines as a boy when sometimes lunch was a cold Butte Pastie. These individual meat pies are good served hot or cold.

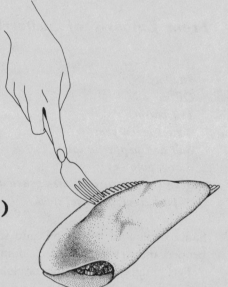

BUTTE PASTIES (Meat Pies)

From Senator Mansfield

DOUGH:

1½ cups flour
½ teaspoon baking powder
½ teaspoon salt

⅓–½ cup shortening
¼ cup cold water (approximately)

Mix all ingredients as for any pie dough. Handle pastry carefully and as little as possible.

FILLING:

1 medium boiled potato, diced
½ pound raw beefsteak, diced
1 cup boiled diced rutabagas (optional)

1 cup chopped onion
Salt and pepper to taste
1 large tablespoon butter

For 1 pastie, take ½ the dough. Roll thin and shape to size of pie plate. Pile ½ the potato, meat, and rutabaga onto only ½ the round of pastry, and to within 1 inch from edge. Sprinkle with onion, salt, and pepper and dot with butter.

Fold other ½ of dough over filling. Press edges together well. Cut slit in top of pastie and pour in 1 teaspoon hot water to keep from drying out. Bake 45 minutes in hot oven (400°) or until well browned, then reduce heat to 350° for 15 minutes. Makes 2 pasties.   SERVES 2 OR 4

AUTHOR'S NOTE: As my dear friend Anne Showell said when she cooked the dish to test it: "Those old Cornish miners were no gourmets. The pasties needed spicing up and were improved with addition of garlic powder and cayenne, or even a little curry. But indeed, they are a welcome change from sandwiches for brown-baggers."

TOM WICKER

Columnist, the New York Times

Tom Wicker has been a newspaperman for twenty-two years, with sixteen of them spent at The New York *Times,* where he is now a columnist and associate editor. He is the author of several books, including his latest novel, *Facing the Lions,* which reached the top of the best-seller list.

The 6'4" 180-pound Wicker has always been fond of eating, but until the experience of being single, he had not experimented in the kitchen. He is an imaginative cook and enjoys complicated and time-consuming recipes, such as his L'Estouffat Lamandé (pot-roasted beef Lamandé), which needs the better part of a day to cook.

When Tom is writing at home, which is often, he frequently takes a break to stir and mix in the kitchen, which helps to give him a new perspective on a difficult passage.

When Tom remarried in 1974, he offered to cook dinner for his bride and her son, Christopher, aged ten. Many hours were spent in the kitchen, and finally a beautiful whole fresh trout, cooked to perfection and adorned with lemon slices and parsley, was presented by a triumphant Tom. Christopher took one long look at the fish which stared back with murky, cooked eyes, and ran upstairs crying. No cajoling and coaxing would persuade him to return.

POT-ROASTED BEEF LAMANDÉ
(L'Estouffat Lamandé)

*From Tom Wicker**

A morsel of beef, massive and tender
  (4 or 5 pounds)
A light farce of truffles, garlic, and
  bread crumbs
1¼ pounds tender carrots, sliced
½ pound mushrooms
¼ pound pitted green olives
1 sweet red pepper

2 fresh pigs' feet
1 fifth beaujolais (a good California
  red works well, and I think a
  bottle and a half goes better)
Salt and pepper to taste
Bouquet garni
Bit of dough

Place the beef, after searing slightly, in a large casserole (I use a large black iron pot with a lid), whose cover can be hermetically sealed.

Apply the stuffing of truffles, chopped garlic, and bread crumbs to the top of the meat. Surround it with carrots, mushrooms, olives, red pepper, and pigs' feet. Pour in the wine. Salt and pepper your morsel and add the bouquet garni. With a long strip of dough, seal the cover of the casserole and cook for 6 or 7 hours (5 or a little more is about right for my taste).

SCALLIONS WITH FRIED PORK (Chinese)

From Senator Nelson

½ pound pork shoulder meat,
  shredded
2 tablespoons soy sauce
1 tablespoon dry white wine

½ pound scallions
5 tablespoons peanut oil
½ teaspoon salt

Mix pork with soy sauce and wine. Cut scallions into 2-inch lengths. Heat oil and sauté pork; when it begins to brown, add scallions and salt. Mix well and cook until scallions just begin to give off juice.

Serve over steamed rice.

SERVES 2

* From *Clémentine in the Kitchen,* by Samuel Chamberlain.

SWEET AND SOUR PORK

From Senator Nelson

1 pound pork tenderloin
2 tablespoons soy sauce
2 tablespoons sherry
1 tablespoon cornstarch
Peanut oil for deep frying
1 teaspoon minced fresh ginger
½ cup coarsely chopped onion
2 tablespoons peanut oil
1 cup tomato sauce
½ cup water or ¼ cup water and
   ¼ cup pineapple juice

⅓ cup sugar
½ cup vinegar
2 teaspoons soy sauce
1 cup bamboo shoots, sliced
1 large green pepper, cut into 1-inch
   squares
1 tablespoon cornstarch
4 tablespoons water

Cut pork into 1-inch cubes. Combine 2 tablespoons soy sauce and sherry and marinate pork for 15 minutes. Stir and drain. Dust with 1 tablespoon cornstarch.

Deep fry pork in peanut oil until golden brown and crisp. With a slotted spoon lift out pork, drain the meat, and keep it warm.

Sauté ginger and onion for 1 minute in 2 tablespoons peanut oil. Add tomato sauce and ½ cup water. Stir in sugar, vinegar, and 2 teaspoons soy sauce. Cook 2 minutes and add bamboo shoots and green pepper. Cook 2 more minutes, stirring constantly.

Combine 1 tablespoon cornstarch and 4 tablespoons water and stir well. Thicken sweet and sour mixture with cornstarch binder. Add the deep-fried pork and heat through, tossing all the ingredients together.

You must stir (toss) the dish all the while you are cooking. If it seems too thick as you cook, add a little water. SERVES 4

GRILLED LEG OF LAMB

From Senator Nelson

"This is a special summer supper at our house."

½ cup soy sauce
½ cup brandy
Freshly ground black pepper

1 leg of lamb, boned and flattened
¼ cup hoisin sauce

Make a sauce of soy, brandy, and pepper. Marinate lamb in the sauce for 4 hours or overnight in refrigerator. Charcoal on hot coals so as to darkly crisp the outside while maintaining a moist, pink inside. Use reserve marinade with hoisin sauce and blend, then brush on lamb during the charcoaling. Remove from grill and cut ½ inch thick on the angle.

DAN RATHER

Author, CBS Correspondent

CBS newsman Dan Rather, at forty-seven, collector of five television Emmy awards, has been at the top of his profession for ten years. He is a hard-nosed, well-informed reporter, experienced in all levels of broadcast journalism. Dan was chief of CBS southwestern bureau in Dallas, where, on November 22, 1963, he waited with television crews to film an anticipated visit between President John F. Kennedy and former Vice-President John Nance Garner on Mr. Garner's ninety-fifth birthday. History canceled the visit, and Rather co-ordinated CBS round-the-clock coverage of the assassination.

Dan likes interesting and foreign dishes and cooks when he has time.

"I like best those foods that remind me of the outdoors and Texas [where he grew up], of campfires and old friends. I also like Chinese, French, and Italian cooking, as well as many traditional Jewish dishes."

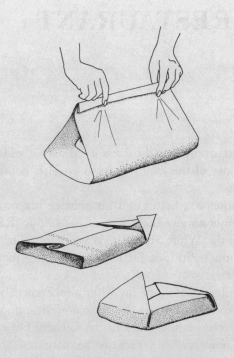

BRISKET OF BEEF WITH SAUCE

From Dan Rather

Sprinkle brisket of beef with celery salt, garlic salt, lemon pepper, and onion salt. Center the meat in a piece of heavy foil, sprinkle with 3 ounces "Liquid Smoke," and fold sides of foil over to seal in packet. Refrigerate overnight.

Six and a half hours before serving, open packet, season with salt and pepper and ½ cup Worcestershire sauce, reseal, and cook in a preheated 300° oven for 5 hours. Uncover and pour over 1 small bottle barbecue sauce. Cook 1 additional hour, uncovered. Let sit 20 minutes before slicing.

Serve with remaining sauce.

AUTHOR'S NOTE: A brisket is usually a skinny piece of beef. I think cooking time of 6 hours is superfluous. The dish was successful when I cooked it 2½ hours in the first oven and 1 hour after adding barbecue sauce. Also, I prefer half the amount of Liquid Smoke called for here. The Liquid Smoke taste and smell are overpowering at first. Finally, the product served hot is not as good as cold. It is quite delicious the next day. SERVES 4–6

SANS SOUCI RESTAURANT

Washington, D.C.

Paul DeLisle left his family's restaurant-hotel business in Marseille when he was thirteen. He didn't want any more of the long 5 A.M. to 10 P.M. hours that his father's business demanded.

Some thirty years later, his hours are better and his prestige has considerably improved. He is maître d', but much more than that, of Sans Souci Restaurant, *the* political place, a block from the White House in Washington. The Capital's leading lawyers, businessmen, and politicians fill the small dining room to capacity daily for lunch and dinner.

Paul is married and speaks affectionately of his wife, also French, who is of course, an excellent cook. Before his marriage, he cooked well and often, but from his wedding day, his wife refused him space in the kitchen. On rare occasions, he prepares a specialty, however, and recently he prepared an elegant *truite Angela* for seventeen close friends. The trout is poached in a bouillon which includes dry white wine and herbs, then the fish is removed and refrigerated, after which the skin is removed and the remaining broth/jelly is spread over the fish. Paul prepared delicate and decorative, also edible, flowers from leaves of leeks. Grated yolk of egg formed the yellow "flower" center and the petals were the carved green leaves of leeks.

What does this expert from one of the world's famous restaurants eat when he is alone? Regardless of how exciting the Sans Souci's menus are, Paul prefers to eat very simply in the restaurant and have his main meal with his wife in their Virginia home. He leaves the restaurant about 4 P.M. and at 4:30 he is relaxed and walking in his garden. His wife often prepares a favorite, *poulet Valée d' Auge,* which should be made in July or August when tomatoes taste like tomatoes, he says. For dessert, he likes *tarte St.-Honoré* or *tarte Tatin.* He recalls the origin of *tarte Tatin.* It seems Madame Tatin made a mistake while cooking in her restaurant kitchen in the French country, and burned the pastry, so she flipped it upside down, and the slightly burned (caramelized) sugar ran through the apples and crust. When her guests asked what she had prepared for dessert, she improvised and said *tarte Tatin,* which is a delicious mistake, indeed.

DeLisle serves fresh orange slices in an unusual way: Slice thin, leave peel on, and dip in caramelized sugar to which butter has been added and heated. Serve warm (page 220).

The French use much imagination in the kitchen. Paul recalls being hungry often during and after World War II and that each potato was carefully peeled and the skins saved. Another meal was created of peels, perhaps an herb or leek added, and *voilà,* a wonderful soup if you are starving.

Sans Souci will not disappoint those looking for a famous face. Senator Eugene McCarthy and Alexis Smith were seen at a table for two; bearded Robert Bork, Solicitor General (now professor of law at Yale), Mrs. William O. Douglas, and Ethel Kennedy are frequent guests. And Art Buchwald's "sources" dine with him nearly every day.

But the restaurant's most notable guests arrived July 14, 1976. Paul points out the corner table where he chose (with the help of the Secret Service) to seat President and Mrs. Ford when the First Lady invited her husband for a birthday lunch. Paul knew twenty-four hours before the President and the public did that the Fords would dine publicly. But discretion is his strong suit and the secret was well kept. He became emotional when he remembered the occasion and the polite behavior of the other diners. They did not stare or intrude and the President and his lady could have a private luncheon in a public place, which could not happen in Europe, he insists. As the President walked into the dining room, everyone burst into spontaneous applause and Paul told the President that he was a good man for having been born in July. The President laughed, patted Paul's shoulder, and said, "You are a good man, too." A special cake had been prepared for the birthday and the waiters, Paul, and all the diners sang "Happy Birthday." (Art Buchwald later accused Paul of arranging the party purposefully when Buchwald was attending the Democratic convention in New York City.) After accommodating the President's party, the Secret Service men, the press table, and the regular diners, Paul was nervous and exhausted. He stepped outdoors to relax with a cigarette. There was no quiet puff, for he opened the door to waiting press, TV cameramen, and hundreds of Washingtonians lining both sides of Seventeenth Street.

And on January 20, 1977, Inauguration Day of another President, the French had their discreet joke. The formal French menu of the Sans Souci Restaurant featured:

Peanut Butter Sandwich, Plains	$ 9.25
Peanut Butter Sandwich, French Style	$10.25

When asked what is "French style" peanut butter sandwich, Paul de Lisle answered, "But of course, with parsley on top."

COLD RABBIT IN TERRINE
(Lapin Froid en Terrine)

From Sans Souci Restaurant

This delicacy calls for a deep, oval clay cooking pot. It should be large enough to hold a whole chicken and it must have a lid with a small hole so that steam can escape. For the fresh bacon use any slices of fresh pork from which fat has been trimmed.

4 slices lean fresh bacon
1 medium rabbit, cut up in medium pieces (supermarkets often have good frozen rabbit)
4 or 5 carrots, sliced about ⅛ inch thick

1 crushed bay leaf
3 tablespoons chopped fresh parsley
¾ teaspoon dried thyme
Salt and pepper to taste
Dry white wine

Put in layers in the clay pot the fresh bacon, pieces of rabbit, layer of sliced carrots, and sprinkle over this some of the seasonings. Repeat the layers until all ingredients have been used. The pot should not be too full. Pour wine over this until liquid covers ¾ of the pot. Cover and seal the lid with thick paste made from flour and water (like paste you would do art work with).

Bake in a preheated 325° oven for about 1½ hours. Allow it to cool in the pot for some hours.

Serve cold. It is an elegant supper dish, and is ideal for an after the theater supper. SERVES 6

HERBERT STEIN

Economist, Author

Economist Herbert Stein is sixty and he has spent the last twenty-two years of his life on various committees for economic development and as chairman of the President's Council of Economic Advisers. He graduated from Williams College magna cum laude, was elected to Phi Beta Kappa, and earned his doctorate twenty years later.

Herbert Stein has written several books on economics and fiscal policy, and with his son Ben a novel about runaway inflation. He is a Senior Fellow at American Enterprise Institute and writes a column for *The Wall Street Journal*.

Dr. Stein's recipe for charcoal-grilled leg of lamb follows. When carefully followed, it is both efficient and delicious.

LEG OF LAMB

From Herbert Stein

1 cup of French dressing (i.e., oil and vinegar according to any cookbook recipe)
⅔ cup chopped onion

2 teaspoons barbecue spice
1 teaspoon salt
¼ teaspoon dried oregano
1 bay leaf, crushed

Have leg of lamb boned and rolled so that it is a flat roll, like doubled over.

For marinade, combine French dressing, onion, barbecue spice, salt, oregano, and bay leaf.

Pour marinade over the lamb which has been placed in a large bowl. Marinate for 1 or 2 days, turning the meat over once or twice. Save marinade.

Meat may be cooked over an open grill. Turn frequently and baste with the marinade. It will take from 45 minutes to 1 hour to cook.

If you are cooking this in the kitchen, put meat fat side up toward the heat, brush well with marinade, and broil 4 inches from the heat until fat becomes golden brown, about 10 minutes. Then turn, baste, and continue to broil another 10 minutes. Set oven control at 450° and bake for 30–35 minutes. Reverse meat for last 5 minutes of cooking. It will be rare and you may want to cook it slightly longer.

Delicious when served with tomatoes and sliced onions which have been made with mustard seed and vinegar.

DR. STEIN ADDS THIS NOTE: "My recipe says that when cooked on the grill the required time is 45 minutes to 1 hour. In fact, you should allow another 1 or 2 hours to get the fire started. In my experience one needs either of two additional ingredients for outdoor cooking. One is a family with a great deal of patience, willing to wait hours for you to get the fire hot enough. Alternatively, they should have a strong tolerance for the taste of lighter fluid, which is likely to overwhelm the marinade if you make an emergency effort to speed up the fire."

BAKED COUNTRY CURED HAM

From the home of Senator Talmadge

Wash country cured ham thoroughly (see note) and put in covered roaster, fat side up. Pour 2 inches of water into pan. (Wine, ginger ale, apple cider, orange juice, pineapple juice, peach pickle juice, Coca-Cola, or champagne may be substituted for the water.) Roast in a preheated 350° oven for approximately 2 minutes per pound or until done. Baste often. When nearly cooked, remove the rind and trim off some of the fat. Score the surface of the fat in diamond shapes and use one of the following glazes:

1. Cover the fat with a paste made of 1 generous teaspoon dry mustard and 1 tablespoon prepared mustard. Pour over ham 1 cup orange juice, pineapple juice, or peach pickle juice and return to hot oven (450°). Uncover. Finish baking. Baste frequently.
2. Stud the diamond shapes with cloves and cover with brown sugar and honey. Add apple cider. Glaze in hot oven (450°), basting frequently.
3. Pour 8 ounces sweet wine over ham and spread with dark molasses. Place in hot oven (450°) for 8–10 minutes. Baste gently and frequently.

Many fine old southern cooks serve their baked hams with the following brandy sauce:

BRANDY SAUCE FOR BAKED HAM

1 pound brown sugar	*Juice of 2 oranges*
6 cloves	*2 ounces brandy*

Mix and heat brown sugar, cloves, and orange juice. Remove from heat and add brandy.

AUTHOR'S NOTE: If you like your ham mild, soak in cold water for 12 hours, depending on age of ham. If ham is very old, would suggest 24 hours.

A country ham usually serves 20.

BONED VENISON SIRLOIN

From Senator Wallop

Take 1 High Plains deer, well killed in late evening. (Mountain deer are not so flavorful but will substitute.) Do not substitute midday deer of any type.

Hang for 2 days (away from dogs and magpies).

Bone same—while pacifying your wife, who must wrap and freeze remainder.

Save *sirloin strip* and cut into 2-inch steaks and butterfly. Season lightly with salt, pepper, and garlic juice. Sauté in 2 tablespoons olive oil (French, not Italian) in very hot pan until medium rare. Never go further; it is tough, dry, and the flavor vanishes.

Serves any number until the loin runs out, but is best with 2 in front of fire after first snowfall.

VEAL WITH MARSALA

From Representative Rodino

2 tablespoons flour	1½ pounds veal scallopini
Salt and pepper to taste	2 tablespoons butter
1 tablespoon chopped fresh parsley	½ cup marsala or sherry
¼ teaspoon dried oregano	¼ cup chicken broth

Combine flour with salt, pepper, parsley, and oregano. Cut veal into 4-inch pieces. Pound seasoned flour lightly into veal. Brown veal well in foamy hot butter. Add marsala and let meat cook another minute. Place meat in serving dish. Add broth to pan and loosen drippings from pan. Pour over veal and serve.

SERVES 2–4

EGGPLANT BOLOGNESE

From Warren Weaver, Jr.

¼ pound smoked ham, sliced
1 cup chopped onion
¼ cup chopped carrot
½ cup chopped celery
4 tablespoons butter
2 tablespoons olive oil
¾ pound finely ground lean beef
¼ pound finely ground pork
½ cup dry vermouth

2 cups beef bouillon
2 tablespoons tomato paste
1 medium eggplant
1 tablespoon Italian herbs
1 teaspoon salt
½ pound chicken livers
1 cup light cream
Salt and pepper to taste
1 cup shredded mozzarella cheese

Chop the ham coarsely and combine on a large cutting board with onion, carrot, and celery, chopping the mixture into very small shreds. Melt 2 tablespoons of the butter in a large heavy skillet over moderate heat and cook the mixture, stirring, for 10 minutes or until lightly browned. Transfer the mixture to a 4-quart pan.

In the same skillet heat olive oil and brown the beef and pork lightly, stirring. Add vermouth, bring to a boil, and stir constantly until the liquid is nearly gone. Add the meat to the ham-vegetable mixture in the pan. Add the beef bouillon and tomato paste, bring to a boil, then reduce heat and simmer, partially covered, for 45 minutes, stirring occasionally.

While sauce is cooking, peel eggplant and cut it lengthwise into slices about 1 inch thick. Bring to a boil enough water to cover the eggplant slices (they will float). Add Italian herbs and 1 teaspoon salt. Simmer eggplant slices for 4 minutes, remove from water, and set aside to drain on paper towels.

Now melt the remaining 2 tablespoons butter in the original skillet over high heat, add the chicken livers, and brown them lightly (about 4 minutes). Remove, drain, and when they are cool enough, chop them into ¼-inch dice. Add them to the sauce after it has cooked for about 35 minutes. When the sauce is ready, add cream, stirring, and bring it back to a low simmer. Add salt and pepper to taste.

In an open Pyrex baking dish, make alternate layers of eggplant slices, sauce, and shredded cheese, saving part of the cheese for a generous over-all topping. Bake in a preheated 350° oven for 20–30 minutes.

Serves 2 amply, maybe 3, depending on the size of the eggplant.

POLISH HUNTER'S STEW (Bigos)

From Warren Weaver, Jr.*

2 pounds sauerkraut (preferably fresh)

3 tablespoons butter

1 cup finely chopped onion

1 teaspoon finely chopped garlic

6 medium mushrooms, coarsely chopped

1 medium tart apple, peeled, cored, and coarsely chopped

2 cups finely shredded cabbage

½ cup dry white wine

2–2½ cups chicken stock, fresh or canned (include in this amount as much pork braising liquid as you have)

1 tablespoon tomato paste

8 dried prunes

Bouquet garni of 6 sprigs parsley, celery tops with leaves, and 1 bay leaf

Salt and freshly ground black pepper to taste

1 pound Polish sausage (kielbasa), cut into 2-inch chunks

½-inch cubes roast fresh ham or pork, to make 1½ cups

2 tablespoons finely chopped fresh dill

Drain sauerkraut, wash it well under cold running water, then soak in cold water for 10–20 minutes depending upon its acidity. Squeeze it dry by the handfuls and put it aside. Ideally, sauerkraut, whatever the dish, should taste only mildly acidulous before being cooked.

Melt butter in a 4-quart casserole that has a heavy tightly fitting cover, and cook onion, garlic, mushrooms, and apple for about 10 or 15 minutes. Stir them frequently and don't allow them to brown. Add the sauerkraut, first gently pulled apart with your fingers, cabbage, wine, 2 cups stock, tomato paste, prunes, and bouquet garni. Mix together gently and bring the liquid to a boil over high heat. Add salt and pepper, cover the casserole tightly, and place it in the center of a preheated 325° oven. Let it cook undisturbed for about 1 hour. If the cabbage seems dry at this point, add the other ½ cup of heated stock. In any case, cook it for ½ hour longer, then bury in the cabbage the Polish sausage and pieces of pork. Cook from 40 minutes to 1 hour longer, and before serving taste for seasoning. In Poland where the making and serving of bigos is as much a ritual as is the serving of choucroute in France, Polish cooks insist that bigos should be served only after it has been reheated and cooled once or twice a day for 3 days. Be that as it may, bigos is every bit as good eaten the moment it is done. Before serving, sprinkle with finely chopped dill.

AUTHOR'S NOTE: Warren Weaver uses cooked *smoked* ham; however bigos can be made, as it frequently is in Poland, with beef pot roast as well as with pork. And often the two meats are combined with fine effect. SERVES 6–8

* From the *Michael Field's Cookbook,* by Michael Field.

BEEF "À LA MODE"

From Embassy of France

Bit of Lard or butter
2 pounds steak, sirloin, rib, or fillet
⅓ cup cognac
½ bottle white wine
1 or 1½ cups beef stock
Calf's foot, cut in half, boned and
    blanched

Few blanched pork rinds
Salt and pepper to taste
Herbs of your choice (bouquet
    garni)
8 small onions
1 cup cut-up carrots

Lard or butter the steak and brown it in a heavy pot over hot fire. Drain off the fat and reserve it for later use. Add cognac to steak in pan and set fire to it; then add mixture of wine, stock, and water to cover the meat. Add calf's foot and pork rinds, which will make the sauce more gelatinous. Add seasonings and herbs. Cover and simmer in preheated 350° oven for ½ hour. Add onions and carrots and cook until vegetables and meat are tender. Remove some of the fat from the sauce, add thickening, and serve in the pot with potatoes or other vegetables.   SERVES 4–6

BENNETT JOHNSTON

Senator from Louisiana

Senator Bennett Johnston of Louisiana is a relative newcomer to Washington. He left his Shreveport law firm for Washington in 1972 to complete the term of the late Senator Allen Ellender.

Mary Johnston is a down-to-earth wife and mother who loves to cook. Although Bennett does the barbecuing when they entertain informally out of doors, the burden (or joy) of cooking falls to Mary. Mrs. Johnston says that "Bennett is a delight to cook for. He is interested in all foods and enjoys trying new ones." Both of them favor plenty of vegetables and dishes that are Louisiana specialties, such as Jambalaya, Shrimp Creole, red beans and rice, and gumbo.

JAMBALAYA

From the home of Senator Johnston

The word "Jambalaya" no doubt derives from the French word *jambon,* which translates ham. The dish varies from kitchen to kitchen, says Mrs. Johnston. It was invented to use leftovers. It is necessary to have chicken, shrimp, sausage, and ham; any one of these can be omitted, but, of course, using all of them makes a more delicious dish.

1 2½–3-pound chicken
1 onion
2 stalks celery
Tabasco sauce to taste
5 scallions, cut up
1 onion, coarsely chopped
1 green pepper, cut up
2 cloves garlic, mashed
½ cup coarsely chopped celery
1 or 2 cups cubed ham
1 pound shrimp
4 or 5 cooked Italian sausages (use mild or hot, not extra *hot)*

3 cups chicken stock
1¼ cups rice
2 or 3 tablespoons chopped fresh parsley
Salt and pepper to taste
1 or more teaspoons Worcestershire sauce
Generous pinch thyme
Taste of tomato ketchup
Few drops Louisiana hot sauce
1 pint canned oysters, drained (or fresh oysters if you are fortunate) (optional)

Boil chicken until tender in water seasoned with whole onion, celery stalks, and Tabasco. Bone the chicken and cut into chunks. Strain and reserve the stock.

Simmer chopped onions, pepper, garlic, and chopped celery for a few minutes in a large heavy pot with cover (Dutch oven is fine). Add cubed ham, shrimp, and chunks of sausage (grease should be sautéed out and discarded, first). Add about 3 cups chicken stock, rice, parsley, salt and pepper, Worcestershire, thyme, ketchup, hot sauce, and the chunks of chicken.

All this should steam for 1 hour or so. It can be done in the oven, but I prefer to cook it on top of the stove, adding water occasionally, so it won't stick.

Oysters may be added during the last 10 minutes of cooking.

Jambalaya is a thick meaty concoction which is considered a main course. It can be served with salad and French bread.   SERVES 8–10

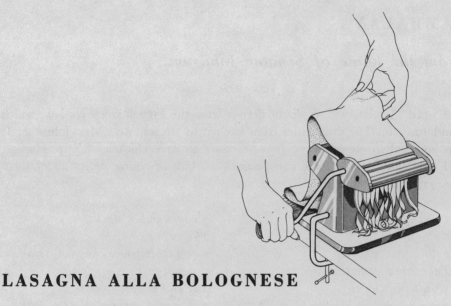

LASAGNA ALLA BOLOGNESE

From the home of Senator Moynihan

BOLOGNESE SAUCE:
- 2 tablespoons butter
- 1 cup chopped onion
- ½ cup chopped carrot
- ½ cup chopped celery
- ¼ pound diced ham
- ¾ pound chopped beef
- 2 tablespoons tomato paste
- 1 cup chicken broth
- ½ cup dry white wine or vermouth
- 1 teaspoon salt
- Freshly ground black pepper to taste
- ½ teaspoon dried thyme

WHITE SAUCE:
- 4 tablespoons butter
- 4 tablespoons flour
- 1 teaspoon salt
- ¼ teaspoon white pepper
- Dash nutmeg
- 1 cup hot milk
- ¾ pound (approximately) mozzarella cheese, sliced
- ¾ cup grated Parmesan cheese

The Bolognese Sauce: In a large pan melt butter over low heat. Add onion, carrots, and celery and simmer about 7 minutes. Add ham and beef, stirring to mix, and cook another 5 minutes.

In a separate bowl mix together tomato paste, broth, wine, and seasonings. Add to meat mixture and simmer 20 minutes. Correct seasonings.

The White Sauce: Prepare as you would any cream sauce: Use low heat, melt butter, and slowly blend in flour and seasonings, stirring constantly for 2 minutes. Remove from heat and stir in hot milk. Return to heat and stir with wire whisk until sauce begins to boil, then turn down heat and continue cooking for about 1 minute.

To assemble the casserole: Prepare homemade lasagna noodles from Green Spaghetti (page 145), or if you wish substitute ¾ pound brand-name lasagna noodles, which have been cooked in boiling salted water until they are *al dente,* neither too soft, nor too hard and uncooked.

Using a heavy square or rectangular lasagna pan, layer some of the meat sauce lightly on the bottom. Add the cooked noodles, more bolognese sauce, and ½ the white sauce. Repeat the layers until ingredients are used up. Top the dish with layers of mozzarella and Parmesan. Cook in a preheated 400° oven for 25–35 minutes.

Let the dish sit a bit before cutting in squares and serving.   SERVES 6

Mrs. Moynihan has found that her Cuisinart makes preparation of the dish "a breeze" and she often quadrupled the recipe when serving large groups of students.

AUTHOR'S NOTE: This is a great dish, but it is a lot of work for 1 small dish which serves 6. My advice is to make several dishes while you are at it and serve to many, or freeze some of the casseroles. However, I agree with Mrs. Moynihan that "I almost never freeze anything." I have never found any frozen dish that was as good as a freshly cooked one.

LAMB IN MARINADE

From David Halberstam

1 cup soy sauce
2 onions, coarsely chopped
3 cloves garlic, mashed

1 leg of spring lamb, boned and
opened flat like a butterfly

Make a marinade of soy sauce, onion, and garlic. Put lamb in the marinade and leave it for a few hours. Remove from marinade and charcoal the meat. It should be dark or slightly burned on the outside and beautifully pink inside.

The lamb can also be seared under the broiler, then roasted in a 300° oven at 15 minutes per pound.

VEAL SHANKS STEIN

From Herbert Stein

2 veal shanks, sliced into 1½-inch
  rounds
3 tablespoons butter
3 tablespoons peanut oil
¾ cup finely chopped carrot
½ cup finely chopped onion
½ cup finely chopped celery
1 clove garlic, minced

3 sprigs parsley, pinch dried thyme,
  and 1 bay leaf (bouquet garni)
Salt and freshly ground black
  pepper
¾ cup dry white wine
1 cup beef broth or consommé
1 cup canned french peas

Brown veal rounds on all sides in hot butter and oil. Transfer them to a heavy kettle or Dutch oven. Sprinkle over them the vegetables, seasonings, wine, and broth; cover and cook over low heat until veal is tender, about 2 hours. Transfer to a warm serving platter.

To the liquid in the pot, add the peas and heat through. Pour the sauce over meat.

Serve with noodles or rice (I use green noodles).   SERVES 6

AUTHOR'S NOTE: The first three vegetables may be combined in a blender with the wine and broth, easing considerably the task of chopping them.

STEWART RICHARDSON

Editor in Chief of Doubleday

Stewart Richardson, known as Sandy, is editor in chief of one of the world's largest and most prestigious publishing houses, Doubleday & Company. Before coming to Doubleday eleven years ago, he was vice-president of J. B. Lippincott Company and worked in early years at Houghton Mifflin. He was graduated from Washington and Lee University in Lexington, Virginia, and earned a master's in comparative literature from Columbia University.

The soft-spoken, confident, sophisticated (but disarmingly shy) Richardson handles his authors with charm and grace. He often employs a useful technique to help execute all these accomplishments—the wonderful business lunch in an excellent restaurant. The conversation becomes easy and the details get worked out over a nice bottle of Brouilly Château de Lachaize 1976 and a delicious entree in one of the many good little French restaurants near Doubleday.

Sandy is an excellent cook and he and his wife, Sally (who works for St. Martin's Press), often cook together at home. Below he has supplied two of his favorite recipes.

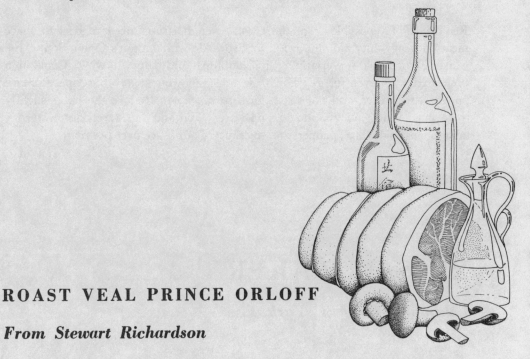

ROAST VEAL PRINCE ORLOFF

From Stewart Richardson

4 pounds veal, rolled and trussed
Olive oil and butter for sautéing
1 pound fresh mushrooms
1 tablespoon soy sauce (light)

3 cups white wine
1 cup water mixed with 2
*   tablespoons cornstarch*
Salt and pepper to taste

Brown veal in mixture of half butter and half olive oil. Put in a preheated 375° oven for 1½ hours.

Remove stems from mushrooms, pulverize caps in a blender, and add soy sauce, wine, and water-cornstarch mixture. (Do not use this all at once—add ¹⁄₁₆ at a time.) Simmer this sauce until it is reduced. Add salt and pepper (scant) and set aside.

Remove veal from oven; cut trusses and discard. Pour the hot mushroom sauce over the veal, reserving some in a gravy boat.

Serve on hot plates, with Vichy Carrots (page 149) and rice or noodles.

SERVES 6–8

FOIL POT ROAST

From Stewart Richardson

1 4–5-pound top round, or chuck roast, rolled and trussed	*1 tablespoon cornstarch*
	Pepper
1 packet Lipton's Onion Soup Mix	*1 or 2 dashes soy sauce or*
1 cup red wine	*Worcestershire sauce*

Remove all fat possible from the roast—even if strings need to be cut. Place meat on heavy-duty aluminum foil and sprinkle with Lipton's Onion Soup Mix. Make French fold—overlapping foil on top—and pour in wine. Cook in a preheated 350° oven for 2–3 hours. Remove, allowing steam to escape. Remove pot roast to platter, and pot roast juices to saucepan. Reduce the juices slightly to ¾ cup (if not enough, add ½ cup water) and add cornstarch dissolved in 3 tablespoons cold water, pepper, and soy sauce. Pour sauce over pot roast.

SERVES 8

RUSSELL BAKER

Columnist, the New York Times

Russell Baker, columnist for the New York *Times,* is a lovely man, slim, tall, handsome, quiet, low-key, and rather shy. Most of the time he seems serious; that is, he doesn't go around grinning and telling jokes as one might suspect America's leading humorist would. Sometimes his writing comes very hard and his office door will be closed all afternoon. Or he will emerge to pace around the *Times*'s corridors until his thinking is freed up. Once based in Washington, Russ tired of trying to find humor in the federal government, particularly Watergate, and in 1975 he and his wife, Mimi, moved to New York. He now writes about crime, Con Ed, garbage, and other amusing subjects. He is also writing plays.

Russ says he "enjoys eating, but as for cooking, I'm more of a beans-and-hot-dogs-over-an-open-fire-man. Mimi accuses me of critiquing the meal." Which is to say, he lets it be known if the food is *not* exceptional, but doesn't always remember to praise when it is. Below is the Bakers' recipe for Veal Scallopini.

VEAL SCALLOPINI

From the home of Russell Baker

1 pound veal, thinly sliced for
   scallopini
Milk
Salad oil

Salt and pepper to taste
Melted butter
1 pound fresh mushrooms
¼ cup dry vermouth

Soak the thin veal slices for 1 hour with milk to cover. Discard milk. Dry meat on paper towels, brush with salad oil, salt, and pepper, and sauté quickly in melted butter in a fairly hot pan. Remove meat.

Slice mushrooms and sauté for a few minutes in same pan. Add dry vermouth until liquid in pan is about ¼ inch. Put the veal back into the pan with mushrooms and cook with lowest fire possible for about ½ hour.　　SERVES 2–4

POULTRY

ROBERT STAPLETON

North Carolina

Dr. Robert Stapleton is the husband of evangelist Ruth Carter Stapleton, sister of President Carter.

He enjoys several hobbies, but favorites are golf (twenty-five tournament quality golf courses in a fifteen-mile radius) and cooking. With his wife's extensive travels, the job of cooking has fallen to him.

"Cookin' is fun," he said. "I love messing around the kitchen and I'm always experimenting. We make our own barbecue sauce and often cook Brunswick Stew. It is a North Carolina specialty and we make a big pot and freeze some for other Sunday night suppers. It should be served with coleslaw and light bread." (In North Carolina light bread is a roll or biscuit—bread made with white flour and yeast or baking powder, not a heavy bread, such as corn bread.)

AUTHOR'S NOTE: An authentic North Carolina barbecue sauce recipe is found on page 196.

BRUNSWICK STEW

From Robert Stapleton

1 5-pound pork roast
1 3½-pound chicken
1½ 1-pound cans corn
2 1-pound cans tomatoes
1 12-ounce bottle tomato ketchup
½ bottle Worcestershire sauce
4 tablespoons prepared mustard

Juice of 3 lemons
1 tablespoon Louisiana (or other) hot sauce
½ cup vinegar
½ cup sugar
1 tablespoon salt
1 tablespoon pepper

Boil pork in several cups water until tender, about 2 hours. Boil chicken in several cups water until tender, about 1½ hours. It is ideal when the cooking water of both pots is nearly evaporated by end of cooking time. Remove the meats from their broths; take meat from bones. Discard broth (or save for another use) and coarsely grind or chop the 2 meats. (Cuisinart is excellent for this.)

Put remaining ingredients in a large heavy pot, add the meat, and simmer together for 4 hours. The finished dish will be a thick stew.

AUTHOR'S NOTE: Brunswick Stew is named for Brunswick County, Virginia.

SERVES 10

SOUTHERN FRIED CHICKEN

From Craig Claiborne*

1 2½–3-pound chicken, cut into
  serving pieces
Milk
Tabasco sauce
1 tablespoon (or more) freshly
  ground black pepper

1 pound lard
¼ pound butter
All-purpose flour
Salt to taste

Place chicken parts in a mixing bowl and add milk to cover. Add a few drops Tabasco and about ½ teaspoon pepper. Let stand 1 hour or longer or refrigerate overnight.

When ready to cook, begin melting lard and butter in a large heavy skillet.

Drain the milk off but do not dry the chicken. Place in a large bowl enough flour to coat the chicken; add salt to taste and the remaining pepper. (Remember that the secret of good southern fried chicken is black pepper used liberally and ample salt.) Dredge the chicken parts in the flour.

While the lard and butter are still melting, start to add the chicken pieces, skin side down. Turn the heat to high and cook the chicken until it is appetizingly brown on that side, then turn the pieces, using tongs. Turn the heat down to moderately low and continue cooking the chicken pieces until golden brown on the other side. Cook until the meat is cooked through, 20 minutes or longer. Drain well on paper toweling.

SERVES 4–6

* From *The New York Times International Cookbook,* by Craig Claiborne.

CHICKEN WITH WINE AND VINEGAR
(Poulet au Vinaigre)

From William Rice

3 tablespoons clarified butter (or 2 tablespoons butter and 1 tablespoon cooking oil)

4 cloves garlic, unpeeled

1 2½–3-pound chicken, cut into small serving pieces (see note)

Salt and pepper to taste

1 large or 2 small tomatoes (about ¾ pound), peeled and seeds removed

½ cup mild white wine vinegar (see note)

2 tablespoons chopped fresh parsley

½ cup chicken stock

½ cup dry red wine (preferably beaujolais)

2 tablespoons butter

Heat butter with garlic in a heavy-bottomed pan, large enough to accommodate the chicken in 1 snug layer. After butter has sizzled and sound dies, add chicken pieces. Sauté over medium-high heat until pieces are lightly browned, 5–7 minutes. Salt and pepper liberally.

Meanwhile, chop tomato to a dice. When chicken is brown, add vinegar. Let liquid come to a brisk boil, then add tomato pieces and parsley, stock, and wine. Cover pan and lower heat to a simmer. Cook 15 minutes, turning pieces once.

Remove chicken to a serving dish and keep warm. Skim fat from pan, then boil down juices for 3 minutes or so to reduce volume by ⅓. Remove garlic peel and mash cooked garlic pulp into sauce. Stir, taste, adjust seasoning, whisk in remaining 2 tablespoons butter. Pour over chicken and serve at once.

Serve with rice. SERVES 4

AUTHOR'S NOTE: Chicken should be cut into 4 leg and 4 breast pieces. First 2 sections of each wing should be cut apart and used. Reserve tips and other less desirable pieces for soup or stock.

Most commercial vinegars are too harsh for this dish. A mixture of ⅔ dry white wine or beaujolais that has begun to turn and ⅓ vinegar will give a better result.

WILLIAM BROCK

Former Senator from Tennessee

Senator William E. Brock of Tennessee lost his Senate seat in 1976, having served his state in the U. S. House of Representatives and Senate for fourteen years. He then became chairman of the Republican National Committee.

His father and grandfather were solid Tennessee Democrats, but he rejected their politics and supported Richard Nixon in 1960. Before his political years he was vice-president for the family business, the Brock Candy Company.

Muffie Brock says, "Bill is the cook and I am the assistant." She recalls that her husband had to come home from the office to roll and flip the crepes suzettes for a Senate wives' luncheon.

Senator Brock's friends rate him a superb cook; his salad dressing is described as "incredibly delicious" and he creates a perfect chocolate mousse. However, when pressed to say what he enjoys cooking he lists three favorites: hollandaise sauce, Tennessee country ham, cooked in an unusual way, and Chicken and Brandy.

Country ham is first favorite with Senator Brock and he shares his method of soaking and cooking it. But don't burn the ham as he did recently when preparing one to serve a party for his staff.

Here is Senator Brock's Chicken and Brandy recipe.

CHICKEN AND BRANDY

From Senator Brock

1 young frying chicken, cut up	2 tomatoes
3 tablespoons butter	1/2 cup dry white wine
1/4 pound fresh mushrooms, sliced	1/2 cup beef consommé
Pinch marjoram	1 tablespoon chopped fresh parsley
Thyme to taste	2 tablespoons minced onion
Salt and pepper to taste	1 ounce brandy

Brown pieces of chicken in butter in heavy skillet with a quick fire. Add mushrooms, marjoram, and thyme. Add cut-up tomatoes and cook 5 minutes. Add wine, consommé, salt, and pepper.

Cook slowly, covered, until chicken is tender, about ½ hour. Remove chicken pieces when they are done. Add parsley and onion and cook about 10 minutes. Remove from heat and add brandy, but do not reheat. Return chicken to sauce and serve.

AUTHOR'S NOTE: Brown rice is a good companion to this dish or use white, as there is a generous sauce.   SERVES 4–6

TURKEY OR CHICKEN IN CREAM

From Clifton Daniel

2 cups cut-up cooked turkey or
   chicken
1 ½ cups cream
2 cups béchamel sauce

2 egg yolks, beaten
Seasonings: grated onion, dash
   celery salt, salt and pepper
Parmesan cheese (optional)

Simmer, but do not boil, the cut-up turkey in cream until the cream is reduced, about ½ hour. Add to the turkey in cream, béchamel sauce, egg yolks, and seasonings. Stir this together very carefully and pour mixture in a flat baking dish or shallow casserole. (The creamed turkey can be put in middle of a ring of rice or mashed potatoes or noodles.) Put the dish under the broiler for 2 or 3 minutes before serving. If you have sprinkled grated Parmesan on top, this will become a golden brown. One should not be heavy-handed with the cheese, however, as it will diminish the delicate flavors of turkey and cream.   SERVES 4

AUTHOR'S NOTE: The Daniels always serve this dish on the day after Thanksgiving.

JAMES BUCKLEY

Former Senator from New York

Senator James Lee Buckley represented New York for one term from 1970 to 1976.

During his Senate years, Senator Buckley became an articulate and effective speaker and was in demand as such. He presently is a commentator for the Westinghouse Broadcasting Company. His natural warmth and good humor make him a popular public person.

For exercise, he hikes, and is a veteran of two Arctic scientific expeditions.

One of his favorite foods, Chicken Florentine, was discovered in an unusual way: His wife found the recipe in a book and was amused that it was attributed to him. She tried it, and has used it for family and dinner parties ever since. Later she found out the recipe belonged to one of the senator's aides.

CHICKEN FLORENTINE

From Senator Buckley

2½–3 pounds chicken pieces
Salt and pepper
2 tablespoons vegetable oil
1 15-ounce can tomato herb sauce
½ cup dry red wine
1 cup uncooked rice
1 2¼-ounce can ripe olives, sliced
1½ cups boiling water

2 10-ounce packages frozen chopped
    spinach, thawed and drained
1 cup ricotta or cottage cheese
1 egg
¼ teaspoon nutmeg
½ teaspoon marjoram
¼ cup grated Parmesan cheese

Season chicken with salt and pepper; brown in skillet in oil. Combine tomato herb sauce and wine. In lightly oiled 3-quart baking dish, combine 1 cup tomato sauce mixture with rice, olives, 1 teaspoon salt, and boiling water; arrange chicken over all. Cover dish tightly with foil. Bake in a preheated 350° oven for 45 minutes.

Meanwhile, press spinach very dry; combine with ricotta, egg, nutmeg, marjoram, and ½ teaspoon salt. Remove foil from baking dish, spoon spinach mixture around edges of dish, and pour remaining tomato herb mixture over center. Sprinkle with Parmesan. Continue baking, uncovered, 10–15 minutes.

SERVES 4–6

AUTHOR'S NOTE: With apology to Senator Buckley and his aide, I think this dish is better if the rice is not put into the sauce and cooked with the chicken, but cooked and served separately.

CHICKEN WITH CREAM AND TARRAGON

From the home of Russell Baker

⅓ cup dry tarragon or 2 handfuls
   fresh tarragon sprigs
2 2½-pound chickens
Salt
1 cup dry white wine
⅓ cup cold water
2 medium onions, cut in eighths
1 stalk celery, coarsely chopped
3 tablespoons butter

4 tablespoons flour
½ cup heavy cream
Juice of ½ lemon
2 egg yolks, beaten
½ pound fresh string beans, cooked
   and drained, or 1 10-ounce
   package frozen, cooked and
   drained

If using dried tarragon, put in cheesecloth bag and place in chicken cavities. Stuff in fresh tarragon without cheesecloth. Salt the chickens and put into deep, not too large casserole. Add wine, water, onions, and celery. Cover and cook in a preheated 400° oven for 1 hour (until juice runs clear, not pink).

To prepare sauce, lift chickens from casserole and strain the remaining liquid (ideally 1½ cups) into a saucepan. Discard what is in the strainer. Make a *beurre manié* by blending butter and flour until smooth. Carefully stir in the *beurre manié* until the liquid thickens. Sauce should not be thick. Add cream and lemon juice and simmer for a few minutes. Stir the sauce gradually into beaten egg yolks. Add beans to sauce and pour it over the chickens.

SERVES ABOUT 6

CHICKEN PARMESAN

From Representative Montgomery

1 cup bread crumbs
½ cup grated Parmesan cheese
¼ cup chopped fresh parsley
1 teaspoon salt
1 clove garlic, mashed

Crushed dried red pepper to taste
6 chicken breasts
1 stalk celery, chopped
1 small onion, chopped
¼ cup butter, melted

Mix bread crumbs, Parmesan, parsley, ½ teaspoon salt, garlic, and red pepper. Let stand for several hours or overnight.

Debone chicken. Boil chicken bones, celery, onion, and remaining ½ teaspoon salt in small amount of water for ½ hour (adding water if necessary) to make a broth.

Roll each chicken breast in melted butter and then in the crumb mixture, covering completely. Roll up and bake for 1 hour in a preheated 350° oven, basting several times with the chicken broth.   SERVES 4

POLLO VILLA RUA

From Embassy of Great Britain

Frozen sweet corn, cooked, or
*   canned, drained (optional)*
2 cups medium thick béchamel
*   sauce*

Leftover cooked chicken pieces
Bread crumbs
1 egg, slightly beaten

Add corn to cooled béchamel sauce if you wish and dip chicken pieces in the sauce. Mix bread crumbs with egg and roll the coated chicken in it. Bake in a preheated 350° oven until golden brown.   SERVES 4–6

FRANK CHURCH

Senator from Idaho

Senator Church won the American Legion national oratorical contest when he was in high school in Boise, Idaho. Skill in public speaking propelled him into national politics and has made him popular among fellow Democrats—he was the party's keynote speaker at the 1960 convention. He is a lawyer and has been a senator since 1956. He gained much publicity while investigating CIA activities as chairman of the Senate's Intelligence Committee, and as a short-lived contender for the presidential pedestal in 1976.

The senator offered two recipes, his favorites. One is called Dressed-up Hamburger but it is not an exciting recipe. His Basque Chicken is good.

BASQUE CHICKEN

From Senator Church

4 whole chicken breasts (or cut-up
    pieces of fryer-broiler)
Flour for dusting
1 medium onion, thinly sliced
4 tablespoons corn oil
1 bay leaf
Thyme to taste

Salt to taste
Coarsely ground black pepper to taste
1 28-ounce can tomatoes, cut up
1 green pepper, thinly sliced
1 8-ounce can mushroom stems and
    pieces or 1 cup fresh
¼ cup stuffed green olives

Cut chicken breasts in half and lightly dust with flour. Fry until golden brown in 2 tablespoons of the corn oil. Place in ready-to-serve casserole.

Brown onion (and mushrooms, if fresh) in remaining 2 tablespoons corn oil. Add bay leaf, thyme, salt, and black pepper. Add tomatoes and let simmer until cooked down a bit. Then add green pepper, mushrooms (if canned), and olives.

Pour this sauce over chicken pieces and bake in a preheated 300° oven for 1 hour.   SERVES 4

WARREN WEAVER, JR.

Reporter, the New York Times

Warren Weaver, Jr., is a lawyer and a newspaperman. He has been writing for the New York *Times* for nearly thirty years, covering New York politics, national politics, and the Supreme Court. He is the author or coauthor of several books, including *Making Our Government Work, Both Your Houses,* and *The Kennedy Years.* He is warm and witty and displays an excellent sense of humor. He is well liked by his colleagues.

Warren learned to cook when his family went to church and he was left alone on Sundays to "put in the roast." He began experimenting and soon found that he spent Sundays in the kitchen by choice.

He is one of Washington's most skilled and most popular cooks. He lives in Georgetown with his second wife, Marianne Means, a lawyer and a columnist, and invitations to their dinners are coveted. Warren not only talks good food and is a careful cook, but he is one who dares to improvise. He can turn a basic recipe into an exciting gourmet treat by adding to it his own special touch. His Chicken Tetrazzini, which follows, is such a dish.

CHICKEN TETRAZZINI

From Warren Weaver, Jr.

6 cups chicken pieces, breasts and
  thighs
2 onions, studded with 2 cloves
4 stalks celery
2 carrots
2 tablespoons salt
1 bay leaf
6 cups water
¼ pound butter
½ cup (or more) flour
Tabasco sauce to taste

1 cup light cream
½ cup dry white wine
2 or 3 cloves garlic, chopped
18 sprigs parsley
1 pound mushrooms, thinly sliced
6 tablespoons butter
1 pound egg noodles
½ cup grated Parmesan cheese
Dots of butter
Sliced almonds

Put chicken, onions, celery, carrots, salt, and bay leaf in water in a large kettle, bring to a boil, and simmer until tender. Remove chicken and skin and bones. Break chicken into rather large bite-sized pieces and reserve. Reduce broth to 2 cups of liquid by boiling. Strain broth.

Melt ¼ pound butter in a saucepan, add flour, and stir with a whisk until blended. Bring broth to a boil and slowly add it to the roux, whisking until smooth. Add Tabasco. Remove from heat and stir in cream and wine.

Sauté garlic, parsley, and mushrooms in 6 tablespoons butter until mushrooms are limp.

Cook noodles according to package directions. Do not overcook.

Put into a large casserole dish in layers the noodles, chicken, mushroom mixture, and sauce.

Add Parmesan and dots of butter.

Sprinkle with sliced almonds. Bake in a preheated 350° oven, covered, for 10 minutes, and uncovered under the broiler for 5 minutes until top is toasty and bubbly and a nice golden color.   SERVES 8

CHICKEN BREASTS

From Warren Weaver, Jr.

6 *chicken breasts, boned and skinned*	6 *tablespoons butter*
4 *tablespoons lemon juice*	3 *tablespoons olive oil*
Salt and pepper to taste	⅓ *cup vermouth*
1 *pound mushrooms*	1 *cup cream*

Sprinkle chicken breasts with 2 tablespoons of the lemon juice and salt and pepper.

Sauté mushrooms in butter and oil for a few minutes, add chicken breasts, and sauté for 1 or 2 minutes on each side.

Put into a covered skillet and bake in a preheated 450° oven for 7 minutes. Remove chicken and keep warm. Add vermouth to skillet and boil liquid down. Add cream and reduce to thick sauce. Return chicken breasts. Add remaining 2 tablespoons lemon juice and additional salt and pepper.   SERVES 4–6

CHICKEN WITH VERMOUTH
AND BLACK CHERRIES

From the home of Ambassador Keeley

5 chicken breasts, split or 10 pieces
   chicken, both dark and light meat
Butter for sautéing
1 cup minced onion

1 cup minced celery
1 cup dry vermouth
1 can pitted black cherries
Salt and pepper to taste

Sauté chicken in butter in Dutch oven or other heavy casserole until golden. Remove chicken and set aside. In same butter, plus a little more, sauté very slowly onion and celery until very tender. Return chicken to casserole, pour over vermouth and about ½ cup of the juice drained from the cherries. Add salt and pepper. Scrape and stir the butter and juice to blend them well. Bake in a preheated 350° oven for about 1 hour. Shortly before serving add drained cherries and continue cooking until cherries are just heated.   SERVES 6

CLAY POT CHICKEN

From David Halberstam

"Goddamn clay cooker is wonderful," says Halberstam.

1 young chicken
Handful green beans
3 tomatoes, cut in thirds
6 small young onions
8 small new potatoes

1 clove garlic, mashed
Small handful fresh basil, cut up
2 teaspoons soy sauce
½ cup dry white wine
Salt and pepper to taste

Put chicken in clay pot, surround it with remaining ingredients, cover the pot, and put it in a cold oven. Turn heat to 450° and cook the dish 1½–1¼ hours. Serve in the pot.   SERVES 4–6

AUTHOR'S NOTE: For any clay pot cooking, the pot and its cover should be soaked in cold water for 10 minutes before putting the food in. Always put the pot in a cold oven.

CHICKEN FROM THE AUGE VALLEY
(Poulet Valée d'Auge)

From Sans Souci Restaurant

1 pound chicken thighs
3 tablespoons butter
1 soupspoon cognac
1 cup chicken broth
2 cups dry white wine
Salt and pepper to taste

3 scallions, tops only, finely chopped
½ green pepper, finely chopped
2 or 3 leaves lettuce, finely chopped
1 tablespoon watercress, finely chopped (optional but excellent)
½ cup heavy cream, whipped

Sauté chicken in butter until golden brown. Remove chicken from pan. Discard fat without scraping the pan. Return chicken to pan and, with medium heat, warm pan 1 or 2 minutes. Sprinkle cognac in pan, put a match to it, and flame it. When flame has subsided, add chicken broth and white wine, salt and pepper, scallions, green pepper, lettuce, and watercress. Be careful to just sprinkle the chopped greens on top of the chicken—do not let them float in the broth, if possible. Your pan should be of sufficient size so that the broth does not cover top of chicken; if it does, pour away some liquid.

Cover, do not stir, and cook slowly about 45 minutes. If the sauce seems runny, carefully remove chicken pieces and cook sauce down a bit. Finally, dilute sauce with whipped cream, put chicken back in, and serve at once.

CHICKEN PICCATA

From the home of Ambassador Buchanan

4 chicken breasts, deboned
Salt and pepper to taste
Flour
1 egg, beaten

½ cup bread crumbs
½ cup grated Parmesan cheese
2 tablespoons butter
2 tablespoons cooking oil

Cut each half chicken breast into 2 slices (making 16 in all). Pound the slices. Season with salt and pepper. Dip in flour, then the beaten egg. Now dip the slices in a mixture of bread crumbs and cheese. Brown slightly in oil and butter. Put in a large flat pan (like a cake pan), cover with foil, and bake in a preheated 300° oven for ½ hour. Remove foil for the last 10 minutes so the pieces will crisp a bit.   SERVES 4

GAYLORD NELSON

Senator from Wisconsin

Senator Gaylord Nelson has been in politics for thirty years. From the state legislature and governorship of Wisconsin, he took a seat in the United States Senate in 1958.

Both the senator and his wife, Carrie Lee, are excellent cooks, but Gaylord specializes almost exclusively in Chinese cooking. Their interest and education in Oriental cuisine stems from friendship with Gaylord's sister and her Chinese husband. From the first, they passed over the familiar mild Cantonese and plunged into the more exciting and fiery Hunan and Szechuan dishes. They say that they cooked Chinese before it was fashionable and bought Kikkoman by the gallon, as it was not always available in rural Wisconsin.

FRIED CHICKEN WITH WALNUTS (Chinese)

From Senator Nelson

2 cups walnuts
1 pound skinned and boned chicken
    breast meat
1 egg white
1 tablespoon cornstarch
2 slices fresh ginger, minced

6 tablespoons peanut oil
1 tablespoon dry white wine
3 tablespoons soy sauce
1 teaspoon cornstarch mixed with 1
    tablespoon water

Toast walnuts at 300° for 10–15 minutes.

Cut chicken meat in ½-inch cubes and mix with egg white, 1 tablespoon cornstarch, and ginger. Stir-fry in hot oil in wok or skillet for 3 minutes, until chicken changes color. Add wine and soy sauce. Cook 2 or 3 minutes, then add cornstarch-water mixture and walnuts. Mix well and stir to heat through.

Serve over steamed rice. SERVES 2

CHINESE CHICKEN WINGS

From Senator Nelson

6–8 chicken wings
1 cup water
¼ cup soy sauce
¼ cup ginger wine

1 teaspoon minced fresh ginger root
¼ teaspoon hot bean paste or
   minced hot Chinese pepper

Chop chicken wings at joints, discarding the bony tips. Place all ingredients in a heavy saucepan and simmer, covered, until the chicken wings are almost done. Uncover and boil rapidly, stirring constantly until almost all the liquid has evaporated. The sauce that is left should now be thick and just enough to cover the wings well. SERVES 2

CHICKEN MARENGO

From Embassy of France

1 3-pound frying chicken, cut up
Oil for frying
½ cup white wine
2 tomatoes, peeled and crushed
10 small cooked mushrooms
10 slices truffle
⅔ cup thickened natural veal stock
   (or chicken stock)

4 crawfish trussed and cooked in
   wine sauce
4 small fried eggs
Chopped parsley
4 pieces toast, fried in butter

Brown chicken pieces in oil. Drain. Mix the oil in pan with wine. Cook until half of it remains. Add tomatoes, mushrooms, truffle, and stock. Return the chicken to the pot, cover, and cook until it is tender. Put the chicken pieces on a warmed platter, cover with sauce, and garnish with crawfish, eggs, parsley, and toast. SERVES 4–6

AUTHOR'S NOTE: The origin of Chicken Marengo comes from the fact that the cook of Napoleon Bonaparte supposedly invented the recipe and prepared chicken in this fashion on the day of the Battle of Marengo. Marengo is a small village in Italy's Piedmont region, famous for the victory of the French led by Bonaparte over the Austrians on June 14, 1800.

FISH AND SEAFOOD

KENNETH RUSH

U. S. Ambassador

Ambassador Rush left the business world to serve his country. He is a lawyer by training and was a corporate executive with Union Carbide before joining the Nixon Administration. He also held directorships in the American Sugar Company and Bankers Trust Company. He recently served as ambassador to France and the interview was held in the Paris Embassy.

Rush is over six feet tall—a well-built and pleasant, agreeable man. He likes to eat and try new dishes. He spoke enthusiastically of *lapin* (rabbit), which is a delicacy in France, but also spoke longingly of some American foods, particularly southern foods, as he grew up in Tennessee.

In early 1976 his friends Senator Howard Baker and Rogers C. B. Morton sent Rush a large Tennessee country ham. Mrs. Rush was delighted and decided it would be an interesting American addition to one of the embassy receptions. But the ambassador did not agree and asked to have it kept for himself. Daily, he had a serving of the ham, but after a week or so, the meat no longer appeared at mealtime. When the ambassador asked Monsieur Bolard, the embassy chef, for more, the chef explained that it was finished. Rush couldn't believe that he had "eaten the whole thing" and demanded to see the bones. He had to content himself with bean soup made from the remainder.

The Rushes entertained in one of the most beautiful houses in the world situated behind a high wall with locked gates and several doormen on the street of famous and incredibly expensive shops, rue Faubourg St.-Honoré. The reception rooms are the size of ballrooms with Cézanne paintings on long-term loan from the Louvre hanging beside paintings by American artists.

Embassy dining is elegant and formal and a typical menu for lunch is the one shown on the next page, followed by two recipes, as prepared by Chef R. Bolard.

LUNCHEON MENU
AMERICAN EMBASSY, PARIS

January 14, 1976

DÉJEUNER

Loup de Mer Flambé au Fenouil	*Sea Bass with Fennel*
Riz au Safran	*Saffron Rice*
Jambon Braise au Porto	*Ham with Port Wine*
Épinards au Croutons	*Spinach with Croutons*
Salade et Fromage	*Salad and Cheese*
Délice du Roi	*Pastry*

THE WINES

Riesling 1973

Domaine des Comtes de Lupfen

Volnay 1966

SEA BASS WITH FENNEL
(Loup de Mer Flambé au Fenouil)

From Ambassador Rush

1 4–5-pound sea bass, boned and skinned	*1 tablespoon cream or* crême fraîche
½ cup Pastis (French licorice-flavored apéritif)	*Dry bread crumbs*
2 medium onions, finely chopped	*4 shallots, minced*
2 fresh fennel bulbs, finely chopped	*Bouquet garni: parsley, thyme, and bay leaf*
3 tablespoons butter	*½ cup chablis*
½ cup dry white wine	*Fresh bread crumbs (4 slices French-type bread)*
1¼ cups finely chopped mushrooms	*2 tablespoons butter*
2 tablespoons minced fresh parsley	*Juice of ½ lemon*
2 tablespoons Pastis	*Cognac*
2 egg yolks	

Sprinkle bass generously inside and out with ½ cup Pastis. Sauté onions and fennel in wine and butter until transparent. Add mushrooms, parsley, 2 tablespoons Pastis, egg yolks, cream, and dry bread crumbs if mixture is too liquid.

Briefly cook shallots and bouquet garni in chablis.

Place fish on parchment paper, stuff with mushroom mixture, and sprinkle with chablis. Close paper tightly and bake fish in a preheated 375° oven for 50 minutes.

Lightly sauté fresh bread crumbs in 2 tablespoons butter and the lemon juice.

Remove top of paper from fish and coat fish with bread crumbs. Sprinkle with warmed cognac and flame at the table. SERVES 6

AUTHOR'S NOTE: In the luncheon menu (page 102) the bass is cooked outdoors over a fire made with branches of dried fennel, a common French method of cooking sea bass.

SCALLOPS EN BROCHETTES
(Brochettes de Coquilles Saint-Jacques)

From Ambassador Rush

2½ pounds shelled scallops	*1 bay leaf*
1 cup dry white wine	*Rosemary*
2 shallots, minced	*Pepper*
1 clove garlic	*Melted butter*
Parsley stems	*Fresh bread crumbs*
Thyme	*¾ cups cooked saffron rice*

If using fresh scallops wash well and dry. Separate the coral. Cut scallops in half and marinate 1 hour in wine, shallots, garlic, parsley, herbs, and pepper. Drain well and dry. Thread them on 10 skewers by putting the coral between 2 pieces of scallop. Each skewer holds ¼ pound shelled scallops. Salt and pepper them and place on buttered baking pan.

Drizzle melted butter over and grill under low broiler heat, 7 minutes per side, or put in very hot oven.

During this time, mix additional melted butter and some bread crumbs, brown slightly, and pour over skewers. Serve on a bed of saffron rice. Pour melted butter that is left in pan over the skewers.

Beurre Blanc or béarnaise sauce may be served with this recipe. SERVES 10

SOLE REJANE

From Embassy of Great Britain

4 tablespoons butter, melted
½ cup chopped fresh parsley
⅔ cup chopped chives
1 cup dry bread crumbs
½ pound mushrooms, coarsely
  sliced

2 tablespoons butter
⅔ cup dry white wine
⅔ cup water
2 pounds fresh sole (or flounder)

Make a paste of melted butter (do not brown butter), parsley, chives, and bread crumbs. Separately sauté mushrooms in 2 tablespoons butter for 4–6 minutes. Combine wine and water.

Arrange sole fillets in a baking dish. Spread a layer of herb paste, then a layer of mushrooms, and pour wine-water mixture carefully over the fish. Bake in a moderate oven 30–40 minutes.   SERVES 6

AUTHOR'S NOTE: An efficient way to make bread crumbs is to put the dry pieces of bread or toast in a plastic bag, seal it, and roll with a rolling pin.

EDWARD BROOKE

Senator from Massachusetts

Senator Edward Brooke of Massachusetts has thought about running for the presidency, but up to now he has been satisfied with election to the Senate and a landslide re-election.

The six-foot-tall quiet Brooke completed five years in the Army in World War II, attended Howard University, and later received a law degree from Boston University.

Senator Brooke is close to his mother and, in fact, often takes her advice on political matters. She frequently acts as his hostess when he entertains in Washington.

He supplies a recipe which betrays his Martha's Vineyard affinities. As an Islander for some twenty-six years, he can think of nothing better to serve his guests than magnificent boiled lobsters. And how simple to prepare.

LOBSTER

From Senator Brooke

Fill a very large kettle ¼ of the way with water. Add salt and bring to boil. Drop 4 1¼-pound lobsters in head first. Cover and cook for 10 minutes.

In the meantime, melt plenty of butter and prepare a crisp green salad.

When 10 minutes are up, remove the lobsters, crack, and eat!

Serve with a very cool Bâtard-Montrachet or, inflation permitting, a Montrachet!   SERVES 4

SAUTÉED SCALLOPS

From the home of Russell Baker

1 pound scallops, fresh if possible	*1½ sticks butter*
1 cup flour	*Juice of 1 lemon*
1 teaspoon salt	*2 tablespoons chopped fresh parsley*

Drain (don't rinse) scallops and dry on paper towels.

Just before you are ready to cook, toss scallops lightly in flour which has been mixed with salt. Jiggle them around in a sieve to get rid of excess flour.

Heat a large heavy skillet and put in ⅓ stick butter. When butter is sizzling, add ⅓ of the floured scallops. Do not put too many into the frying pan or they will cool down the butter and pan and take longer to cook. If they are over-cooked they are tough. Leave scallops in the hot pan about ½ minute. Turn them over one by one and brown other side. One minute cooks the scallops, ½ minute each side. Put on a warm platter, wipe out the pan with a paper towel, and repeat the process twice more.

Brown the remaining ½ stick butter over medium heat. Squeeze lemon juice over the scallops, pour brown butter over all, sprinkle with chopped parsley, and serve.   SERVES 2

AUTHOR'S NOTE: Have everything ready, as once you start cooking the scallops, time is important.

CLIFTON DANIEL

New York Times

Clifton Daniel has been with the New York *Times* for over thirty years. He was foreign correspondent much of that time serving in the London Bureau and as head of its West Germany and Moscow bureaus. He was managing editor of the *Times,* and later head of the Washington Bureau. He is married to Margaret Truman and they have four sons, ages eleven to twenty. Margaret has completed her fourth book, *Women of Courage,* and is working on three new ones. She travels about the country promoting her books, appearing on TV and radio. Clifton enjoys being with the boys in the evening, and cooking when he has time. Margaret said in a recent interview:

"Clifton is an excellent cook and I hate to cook. I like everything he cooks and never complain as long as I don't have to do it. When Clifton cooks, he is careful, but willing to improvise; his rice salad is different each time. I never ask what is in a dish; if I know, then I might have to make it. Clifton is an expert with veal and often makes veal marsala or scallopini as well as veal with tuna sauce." Margaret Daniel ended the conversation with a familiar phrase: "He is a wonderful cook but he always leaves the pots and pans."

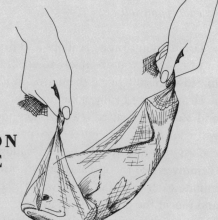

COLD POACHED SALMON WITH SAUCE GRIBICHE

From Clifton Daniel

Fresh salmon is delicate and should not be overcooked. The best method is to place the fish on a fish rack so that it does not rest on the bottom of the cooking pot and it can be easily removed. If you do not have a fish rack, gently wrap the fish in a generous piece of cheesecloth, twisting the ends to form handles, so that the fish can be carefully lifted from the liquid after cooking.

When the fish is laid to rest in an enameled cooking pot, pour cold strained Court Bouillon over it. (See below for Mr. Daniel's Court Bouillon.) Bring to a boil. Simmer for 12–15 minutes. When the fish can be easily pierced with a toothpick or flaked with a fork, it is properly poached.

Allow fish to cool in the cooking liquid. Remove and serve with Sauce Gribiche.

COURT BOUILLON FOR POACHING SALMON

1 cup dry white wine
Fish bones, heads, tails
1 stalk celery, coarsely chopped
1 onion, sliced
2 carrots, coarsely chopped
1 large sprig parsley

1 bay leaf
1 or 2 sprigs each fresh tarragon,
*   rosemary, and thyme (if you must*
*   used dried herbs, tie them in*
*   cheesecloth)*

Add enough water to wine to cover the fish you are cooking. If you don't have fish scraps, just use water and wine. Boil the liquid with all the ingredients for 20 or 30 minutes. Let it cool and strain it.

EASY SAUCE GRIBICHE

1 cup mayonnaise (store-bought
*   mayonnaise will do; homemade*
*   would be better)*
2 tablespoons finely chopped shallot
*   or onion*
¼ teaspoon dried thyme

1 tablespoon chopped chives
1 tablespoon chopped fresh parsley
½ teaspoon dried tarragon (1
*   teaspoon fresh tarragon would be*
*   better)*
1 hard-boiled egg, finely chopped

Mix all ingredients together. Serve with cold poached salmon, cold lobster, cold fish, or cold shrimp.

AUTHOR'S NOTE: Parsley can be chopped in large bunches and stored in the freezer. As you remove it, do not allow unused portion to thaw because it will refreeze in a lump.

AUTHOR'S NOTE FOR POACHING FISH: Several of these recipes call for poaching fish. If you have not done this before, proceed cautiously. First of all, the fish should only simmer gently, not boil in the wine-water liquid. Ideally, one should have a vessel called a fish poacher, but if you do not have one, use a shallow frying pan, and if there is not much liquid, keep spooning it over the fish, as the fish is too fragile to turn over, or increase the liquid to cover the fish. When you think the fish is tender (if it flakes easily), remove it immediately by lifting with 2 spatulas onto a serving dish. Some recipes recommend poaching for 10 or 15 minutes. I personally believe this is too long, as fish would be cooked to a mush in this length of time. Seven minutes is more reasonable.

Secondly, you should not try to use any (or at the very most, 1 tablespoon) of the wine-water poaching liquid in the recipe, as it is too strong. The fish is delicately flavored, and poaching it in the wine gives the dish enough of this flavor.

SHRIMP FRIED IN BEER BATTER

From Clifton Daniel

1 cup flour	*½ teaspoon Worcestershire sauce*
¼ teaspoon salt	*1 tablespoon cognac*
1 egg, beaten	*1 small clove garlic*
1 tablespoon melted butter	*Vegetable oil*
1 cup beer	*⅔ cup mayonnaise*
1 egg white, beaten	*⅓ cup horseradish*
1 pound cleaned shrimp	

Make a batter of flour, salt, egg, butter, and beer. Do this an hour ahead and keep it warm so that it rises and becomes foamy and light with action of the beer. When ready to begin cooking the shrimp, beat and fold egg white into the batter.

Meanwhile, marinate shrimp briefly in Worcestershire, cognac, and garlic juice extracted with a garlic press.

Dip shrimp in batter and give each shrimp a twist to swirl the batter onto the shrimp. Fry in vegetable oil at 375° a few minutes until gold brown.

Combine mayonnaise and horseradish and serve with the shrimp.   SERVES 2–3

AUTHOR'S NOTE: Clifton says, "I borrowed this recipe from Craig Claiborne, and with apologies to him have added and subtracted to suit myself."

POACHED SABLE FISH (or Black Cod)

From Senator Stevens

Poach 8 fish steaks for 10 or 15 minutes in 1 cup or more of wine (I use inexpensive white wine) with a pinch of thyme or tarragon.

Serve the steaks on top of rice and pour melted butter over all, adding salt and pepper.

I usually serve salad as a separate course, after the fish, and make it with several kinds of lettuce, avocado, tomatoes, rutabaga (thinly sliced,) and red onion.   SERVES 6

STROM THURMOND

Senator from South Carolina

Senator Strom Thurmond was originally a farmer from Aiken, South Carolina. He studied law at night and eventually practiced law in his home state. He is admitted to practice in all federal courts, including the United States Supreme Court. He postponed his law career to join the Army on December 11, 1941, the day war was declared against Germany. He won a multitude of honors, awards, and medals, including the Legion of Merit, Purple Heart, and several distinguished foreign decorations.

Senator Thurmond has a similarly outstanding congressional record, having been a senator for nearly a quarter of a century.

But he received more national publicity, not for his war and Senate achievements, but for switching his politics from Democrat to Republican in 1964, for marrying in 1968 (his second marriage) a South Carolina girl forty-four years his junior, and fathering four children in the last eight years.

His favorite food is Crab Cakes, made with fresh South Carolina crabs.

CRAB CAKES

From Senator Thurmond

1 pound cooked crab meat
2 eggs
2 tablespoons mayonnaise
1 tablespoon horseradish mustard
¼ teaspoon salt

⅛ teaspoon pepper
Dash Tabasco sauce
1 tablespoon chopped fresh parsley
1 cup cracker crumbs

Combine all ingredients except cracker crumbs and mix lightly together. Form mixture into 4 cakes or croquettes. Do not pack firmly, but allow the mixture to be light and spongy. Roll out a package of crackers into fine crumbs (do not use prepared cracker crumbs). Pat the crumbs lightly on the crab cakes and fry in deep fat just until golden brown. Remove hot cakes just as soon as golden brown. Drain on absorbent paper and serve hot with a smile! MAKES 4 CAKES

FISH AND SEAFOOD

HUGH SCOTT

Senator from Pennsylvania

Senator Hugh Scott came to Washington in the 77th Congress and was re-elected for seven additional terms until his resignation in 1976. His most prestigious positions were minority leader of the Senate for several years and member of foreign relations and judiciary committees.

He was one of the first prominent Americans to visit the People's Republic of China (at the invitation of Chou En-lai) after President Nixon negotiated diplomatic relations with China, a special thrill because he is a lifelong student and collector of Chinese art.

He is author of several books, and he lectures when he can on politics, art, literature, and life.

The Republican senator, though Pennsylvania's representative, grew up in a small Virginia river town, "where," he says, "seafood was much more of a staple than meat. And soft-shell crabs are out of this world. My favorite food is Crab Meat au Gratin." A recipe for it follows.

CRABMEAT AU GRATIN

From Senator Scott

4 tablespoons butter
5 tablespoons flour
1½ teaspoons salt
2 cups milk
Red pepper to taste
2 tablespoons sherry
½ pound extra-sharp cracker barrel
  cheese, grated

2 pounds cooked fresh crab meat
2 8-ounce cans large mushrooms,
  drained
1 cup cooked shrimp (optional)
¾ cup toasted bread crumbs

Make a white sauce of butter, flour, salt, milk, and red pepper. Add sherry and cheese. Stir in crab meat, mushrooms, and shrimp. Pour into buttered casserole and top with toasted bread crumbs. Bake in a preheated 400° oven for about 20 minutes.   SERVES 8

AUTHOR'S NOTE: Serve over rice; have a green salad.

CRAIG CLAIBORNE

Food Editor of the New York Times

For most of us who like to cook and eat, Craig Claiborne is the ultimate polished palate. He has been food editor for the New York *Times* for twenty years and is quoted as saying that he would not leave for $200,000, that he now has everything he wants.

He would rather cook than eat and has arranged his life so that he usually comes into New York City to the Times Building one or two days a week. The other five or six days are spent in restaurant dining or cooking in the professionally equipped kitchen of his home in East Hampton, Long Island.

Craig is in his mid-fifties and looks ten years younger. He is not fat from all the eating because he takes small portions—tastes, actually. He is carefully and conservatively dressed, pleasant and cheerful, and though he is a serious cook and writer, he does not take himself too seriously. He declares emphatically that he "loves cooking, but hates writing."

Cooking has always been his hobby and now his livelihood. And what does the world's number one critic and connoisseur of fine food eat when he is alone? When he is not entertaining Hamptons friends Lillian Gish, Helen Hayes, Betty Freidan, Betty Comden, Peter Stone, Irwin Shaw, Wilhelm de Kooning, or Jimmy Ernst? What does he eat when he has been extravagantly fed all week and just wants a simple bite? Does he poach an egg like the rest of us? Or prepare something childish and perhaps obsolete—warm milk toast with sugar and cinnamon? He quietly, but emphatically, answered no. He likes to eat good hamburgers and spaghetti and meatballs. And he caters to his health by drinking the juice of one or two grapefruit every day. For breakfast, after the juice, there is a glass of hot clam and tomato juice, spiced with Tabasco. Add a piece of toast. He admitted that his food tastes were odd, but says he is never sick and believes this unusual breakfast is much of the reason. He is not fond of desserts, which he enjoys cooking, but rarely eats them because he can only eat so much and he prefers the main course.

I think his "favorite" dish changes from time to time. One of his good friends who attended a political convention with him in 1968 remembers that his favorite food then was Fried Chicken (fried according to Claiborne, see page 84) but he now gives top place to Coulibiac of Salmon, which is something of a hot salmon pâté, Russian in origin. It consists of brioche dough, stuffed with salmon and rice, and includes a rare ingredient called vesiga, the spinal marrow of sturgeon. (If you have never heard of this before, don't despair. Few food fans have.) The dish is served with a sauce of melted butter.

COULIBIAC OF SALMON

From Craig Claiborne

Brioche Dough (*see recipe*)
Salmon and Mushrooms with
    Velouté (*see recipe*)
14 7-inch crepes
Rice and Egg Filling (*see recipe*)
2 egg yolks, beaten

2 tablespoons cold water
2 tablespoons butter at room
    temperature
¾ pound plus 4 tablespoons hot
    melted butter

BRIOCHE DOUGH

¾ cup milk
¼ teaspoon sugar
3 tablespoons (packages) dry yeast
4–4½ cups flour

Salt to taste
1 cup egg yolks (about 12)
8 tablespoons (1 stick) butter at
    room temperature

Pour the milk into a saucepan and heat it gradually to lukewarm. Remove from heat. If the milk has become too hot, let it cool to lukewarm.

Sprinkle the milk with sugar and yeast and stir to dissolve. Cover with a towel. Let stand about 5 minutes and place the mixture in a warm place (the natural warmth of a turned-off oven is good) about 5 minutes. It should ferment during the period and increase in volume.

Place 4 cups flour with salt in the bowl of an electric mixer fitted with a dough hook, or use a mixing bowl and wooden spoon. Make a well in the center and pour in the yeast mixture, cup of yolks, and butter. With the dough hook or wooden spoon gradually work in flour until well blended. Then beat vigorously until dough is quite smooth and can be shaped into a ball.

Turn the dough out onto a lightly floured board and knead until it is smooth and satiny, about 10–15 minutes. As you work the dough, continue to add flour to the kneading surface as necessary to prevent sticking but take care not to add an excess or the finished product will be tough.

Lightly butter a clean mixing bowl and add the ball of dough. Cover with a clean towel and let stand in warm place about 1 hour. Turn it out once more onto a lightly floured board. Knead it about 1 minute and return it to the clean bowl. Cover closely with plastic wrap and refrigerate overnight.

The next morning punch the dough down again and continue to refrigerate, covered, until ready to use.

SALMON AND MUSHROOMS WITH VELOUTÉ

2 skinless, boneless salmon fillets,
  preferably center-cut, each
  weighing about 1½ pounds
2 tablespoons butter
2 tablespoons finely chopped onion
2 tablespoons finely chopped shallot
Salt and freshly ground pepper to
  taste
¾ pound mushrooms, thinly sliced
¼ cup finely chopped fresh dill
2 cups dry white wine

2 tablespoons butter
3 tablespoons flour
⅛ teaspoon cayenne pepper
3 tablespoons lemon juice
5 egg yolks
Salt and pepper to taste

For the salmon and mushrooms, cut each fillet on the bias into slices, ⅓ inch thick (12 slices per fillet). Rub a 13½×8½×2-inch baking dish with butter and sprinkle with onion, shallot, salt, and pepper. Arrange fillet slices, slightly overlapping on top. Salt to taste, with liberal sprinkle of black pepper. Scatter the mushrooms over the salmon. Sprinkle fresh dill and pour the wine over all. Cover with aluminum foil and bring to boil on top of stove. Place dish in a preheated 400° oven and bake 15 minutes. Remove the dish and pour the accumulated liquid into a saucepan. Spoon off most of the mushrooms and transfer them to another dish. Bring cooking liquid to boil over high heat.

For the velouté, melt butter in a saucepan and whisk in flour. When blended, add the cooking liquid, whisking rapidly. Cook 5 minutes, stirring often. Add the mushrooms and cook 20 minutes, adding any liquid that accumulates around the salmon, which is sitting in the baking dish. Add cayenne pepper and lemon juice. Beat the yolks with a whisk and scrape them into the mushrooms, stirring vigorously. Cook 30 seconds and remove. Salt and pepper to taste. Spoon this sauce—it should be quite thick—over the salmon. Try to avoid having the sauce spill over the sides of the salmon. Cool.

Grease a rectangle of waxed paper with butter. Arrange this, buttered side down, on the sauce-covered salmon and refrigerate until thoroughly cold.

Remove the salmon from the refrigerator. Cut in half lengthwise down the center.

Remove the brioche dough from the bowl and with floured fingers shape it into a thick flat pillow shape. Place the brioche dough on a lightly floured board and roll into a rectangle measuring about 21 by 18 inches. The rectangle should have slightly rounded corners. Arrange 8 crepes, edges overlapping in a neat pattern, over the center of the rectangle, leaving a border of brioche dough.

RICE AND EGG FILLING

3 hard-boiled eggs
1¾ cups firmly cooked rice
¼ cup finely chopped parsley
1 tablespoon finely chopped dill

Salt and freshly ground pepper to
taste
1½ cups chopped cooked vesiga
(optional)

Chop the eggs and add them to a mixing bowl. Add the remaining ingredients and blend well.

Sprinkle the crepes down the center with a rectangle of about ⅓ of the rice mixture. Pick up half the chilled salmon and carefully arrange it, mushroom side down, over the rice mixture. Sprinkle with another ⅓ of the rice mixture. Top this, sandwich fashion, with another layer of the chilled salmon filling, mushroom side up. Sprinkle with remaining rice. Cover with 6 overlapping crepes.

Bring up 1 side of the brioche. Brush it liberally with a mixture of beaten yolks and water. Bring up the opposite side of the brioche dough to enclose the filling, overlapping the 2 sides of dough. Brush all over with egg yolk. Trim off the ends of the dough to make them neat. Brush with yolk and bring up the ends, pinching as necessary to enclose the filling.

Butter a baking dish with 2 tablespoons butter. Carefully turn the coulibiac upside down onto the baking dish. This will keep the seams intact. Brush the coulibiac all over with yolk. Using a small round decorative cookie cutter, cut a hole in the center of the coulibiac. This will allow steam to escape. Brush around the hole with yolk. Cut out another slightly larger ring of dough to surround and outline the hole neatly. Roll out a scrap of dough and cut off strips of dough to decorate the coulibiac. Always brush with beaten yolk before and after applying pastry cutouts.

Roll out a 6-foot length of aluminum foil. Fold it into thirds to make 1 long band about 4½ inches in height. Brush the band with 4 tablespoons melted butter. Arrange the band neatly and snugly around the loaf, buttered side against the brioche. (This band prevents the sides of the loaf from collapsing before the dough has a chance to firm up while baking.) Fasten the top of the band with a jumbo paper clip. Run a cord around the center of the foil band to secure it in place. Run the cord around 3 times and tie the ends. Make certain the bottom of the loaf is securely enclosed with foil. Set the pan in a warm, draft-free place for about 30 minutes. Place the loaf in a preheated 400° oven and bake 15 minutes, then reduce heat to 375° and bake 10 minutes longer. Cover with a sheet of aluminum foil to prevent excess browning. Continue baking 20 minutes. Remove foil and continue baking 15 minutes more (total time, 1 hour). Remove the coulibiac from oven. Pour ½ cup melted butter through the steam hole into the filling. Serve cut into 1-inch slices with hot melted butter on the side.

SERVES 16 OR MORE

AUTHOR'S NOTE: One of the classic, but optional, ingredients for a coulibiac of salmon is vesiga. It is a ropelike, gelatinous substance, actually the spinal marrow of sturgeon. The vesiga, after cleaning, must be simmered for several hours until tender.

SHRIMP CREOLE

From the home of Senator Johnston

½ cup flour
½ cup bacon grease
½ cup water
2 large onions, cut up
8 or 9 small scallions, cut up
1 large green pepper, cut up
2 large cloves garlic, mashed
    somewhat
2 stalks celery, including some
    leaves, chopped somewhat

1 bay leaf
Thyme
Salt and pepper to taste
1 28-ounce can stewed tomatoes
1 8-ounce can tomato sauce
1 or 2 tablespoons tomato paste
1½ cups chicken or shrimp stock
1½ or 2 pounds shrimp
Handful fresh parsley, chopped
2 tablespoons lemon juice

Make a roux (gravy) of flour and bacon grease, adding water to the smooth paste. In an electric blender combine onions, scallions, green pepper, garlic, and celery. Add the blended mixture slowly to the roux as it cooks. Add bay leaf (remove bay leaf before freezing this sauce), thyme, salt, and pepper.

Add tomatoes, tomato sauce, and tomato paste to the roux mixture. Then add chicken or shrimp stock and cook all this about 1 hour. Now add the shrimp, parsley, and lemon juice. If you freeze shrimp creole, do not add the parsley, shrimp, or lemon juice. Simply freeze the sauce and add these ingredients the day you serve the dish. If the shrimp has been frozen, peel it and cook it in the sauce for 3 or 4 minutes, depending on size of shrimp. Shrimp should not be overcooked, as it becomes tough.

Serve over rice.   SERVES 6–8

GREEN PEPPERS STUFFED WITH SQUASH AND SHRIMP

From the home of Senator Johnston

4 or 5 green peppers
2 medium yellow summer squash,
    peeled and sliced into thick rings
1 medium onion, chopped
Bacon grease

1 pound raw or cooked shrimp,
    peeled (see note)
Salt and pepper to taste
Louisiana (or other) hot sauce
Seasoned bread crumbs

Remove seeds and membrane from peppers and put peppers in boiling water until they are soft, perhaps 3 minutes. Overcooking makes them lose color and shape. Drain the peppers.

Peel, slice, and cook the squash in a pot with tight cover a few minutes until tender, in very little water. Perfection is when the water has evaporated at the moment the squash is tender. Mash it with a fork, draining off excess water.

In another pan, sauté chopped onion in a little bacon grease (I don't believe in using a lot of grease, even though southern cooking calls for it.) If time is precious, don't sauté onion, only chop and put in with squash.

Add the cooked squash, then shrimp, salt and pepper, hot sauce, and stuff all this into the green peppers. Put bread crumbs on top and put in a preheated 350° oven in a casserole dish for 15 or 20 minutes.   SERVES 4

AUTHOR'S NOTE: Use small shrimp or cut large ones. If shrimp is frozen, defrost first.

MAURITIAN FISH (Vinday)

From the home of Ambassador Keeley

3 pounds firm-fleshed fish, as
   boneless as possible
1 quart safflower or other oil (oil
   can be saved)
4 tablespoons powdered saffron
1 tablespoon mustard seed
1 ginger root or 1 tablespoon dried
   ginger

4 cloves garlic
1 pound small onions or shallots
4 green chili peppers, sliced
½ cup white vinegar
Salt and pepper to taste

Clean fish, removing skin, bones, etc., and cut into rounds or chunks. Cook immersed in hot oil until lightly browned. Do not overcook or fish will not then properly absorb the spices. Remove fish from oil and save oil.

Mix saffron with a little water to make a paste, then stir for a few seconds in hot oil.

Crush mustard seed, ginger root, and garlic and add to oil with the peeled onions and sliced chilis. Cook less than a minute. Add fish and mix carefully, but well. Vegetables should remain half cooked and crisp. Remove from fire, add vinegar, and mix again. Cover and allow to be undisturbed at room temperature for 12 hours. Refrigerate for 3 or 4 days. To serve, bring back to room temperature. Vinday is served at this temperature.

Serve with hot rice, Mauritian Lentils (page 128), and Mauritian Chutney (page 199).   SERVES 6

SHRIMP AND PESTO SAUCE
FOR SPAGHETTI (Scampi al Pesto)

*From Tom Wicker**

1 pound raw shrimp	*Salt and freshly ground black*
2 tablespoons olive oil	*pepper to taste*
2 tablespoons butter	*3 tablespoons pesto (see recipe)*
Juice of 1 lemon	

Shell and devein shrimp.

Heat oil and butter in skillet. When oil is hot, add shrimp. Cook, tossing frequently, until shrimp turn color. Add lemon juice, salt, and pepper. Continue cooking and tossing about 5 minutes. Add pesto, toss, and cook for several minutes more.

Serve over pasta with salad or sautéed zucchini. SERVES 4

PESTO

2 cups coarsely chopped fresh basil	*6 anchovy fillets, chopped*
1 tablespoon chopped parsley	*Salt and freshly ground black*
1 tablespoon chopped garlic	*pepper to taste*
¼ cup olive oil	

Add all ingredients to blender. Blend, stirring down with a rubber spatula as necessary, until a smooth paste forms. Unless the pesto is to be used immediately, spoon it into a Mason jar or other container and cover with ¾ inch olive oil. Cover tightly and store in refrigerator. It may be kept indefinitely, used any time, spooned directly from jar. MAKES 2 CUPS

* From *Italian Family Cooking,* by Edward Giobbi.

SAUTÉED FLOUNDER

From Ned Kenworthy

4 fillets of flounder
1 ½ cups milk
Flour for dusting
2 tablespoons peanut oil

3 tablespoons butter
2 tablespoons lemon juice
Handful fresh parsley, chopped

Ned Kenworthy says flounder is best prepared by soaking the fillets in milk for 20 minutes, to remove any fishy taste and to prevent curling.

Soak fillets in milk. Discard the milk. Dry fish with paper towel and dust *lightly* with flour.

Fry the flounder in oil barely 2 minutes on each side; turn the fish carefully, as they are fragile. Place (again carefully) on a warm platter and store in oven.

Heat butter, to a light brown, squeeze lemon juice into the butter, add parsley, and pour over the fish. SERVES 2

HARRISON WILLIAMS

Senator from New Jersey

Those who work long hours every day with Senator Harrison Arlington Williams, Jr., of New Jersey, say he is a "kind and fair man with a beautiful disposition."

He has held such diverse jobs as navy pilot in World War II, steelworker, college professor, and practicing attorney. During his twenty years in the United States Senate hc has sponsored legislation on mine safety, benefits for the aged, transportation improvements, and changes in the securities industry.

The senator likes to get up early, often doing his most productive campaigning at factory gates when the workers begin arriving about dawn. He is medium tall with a slim figure, which he maintains with exercise and nutritious food. Jeanette Williams is a good cook who is adamant about serving well-balanced and attractive meals. One of her elegant box lunches goes to the Senate with her husband every day and a perfect meal awaits him each evening.

Says Senator Williams: "Jeanette's Shrimp Mousse is her own creation. I first tasted it at a New Jersey State Society gathering years ago. I was much impressed by its flavor and texture then, and the years between have served to reinforce my original judgment.

"Many interesting guests have partaken of this gastronomic tour de force. On the evening prior to President John F. Kennedy's inauguration, one guest, Vice-president-elect Lyndon B. Johnson, tasted the Shrimp Mousse for the first time and praised it highly."

SHRIMP MOUSSE

From Senator Williams

1 10-ounce can tomato soup
8 ounces cream cheese
1½ tablespoons gelatin, softened in
 ½ cup water
2 4½-ounce cans shrimp

¾ cup chopped onion
¾ cup chopped celery
1 cup mayonnaise
Salt to taste

Bring soup to a boil, add cheese, and beat until smooth and melted. Add gelatin, and cool until slightly thickened. Mash shrimp. Add shrimp, onion, celery, and mayonnaise to soup mixture. Place in refrigerator. Take out ½ hour before serving. SERVES 4–6

PASTA WITH CLAM SAUCE (Spaghetti Vongole)

From Ned Kenworthy

12 hard-shell clams (quahogs) (I
 use middle size, i.e., cherry
 stones)
1 cup dry white wine
2 tablespoons olive oil
2 cloves garlic, chopped

2 or 3 scallions, chopped
Handful fresh parsley, chopped
1 pound pasta (linguine or spa-
 ghetti)
1 cup (or more) grated Romano or
 Parmesan cheese

Wash the clams under the cold water tap (see page 123 for detailed directions on washing and preparing clams).

Put the clams in a pot with wine.

Cover and simmer until clams open (just a few minutes).

Remove from heat. Drain and reserve broth. Strain it.

With a sharp knife, remove clam meat, put it in a wooden bowl, and chop finely with a chopper.

Heat olive oil with garlic until garlic sizzles, then remove it. Put in scallions and parsley and cook 2 minutes. Add chopped clams and wine broth and let all bubble 1 or 2 minutes.

Put drained cooked pasta on heated platter; pour clam sauce and some cheese over the pasta, toss and serve. Serve extra cheese at the table.   SERVES 4

CLIFF ROBERTSON

Actor

Actor Cliff Robertson, star of the movie *Charly* and the one who lost the girl to William Holden in *Picnic,* loves to cook when he has time and in fact taught his wife, actress Dina Merrill, what she knows about the kitchen. The Robertsons work together in the kitchen, particularly in their summer home in East Hampton, "but only one of us cooks and the other does the little things—one chef at a time," says Cliff.

Cliff was born and grew up fishing in La Jolla, California. He had a lobster route as a kid and sold the clawed creatures for fifty cents a pound. He caught abalone by wrapping fishing cord around his wrist. Twenty years later he savors the remembered taste of this fish, breaded and sprinkled with fresh lime juice, then broiled. He always manages to live near the water, and the recipes he talks about are mostly made with sea catches of his own.

He also likes to eat good old favorites like chili. There is nothing better than good chili, he believes, remembering his early acting years when he lived in Greenwich Village in New York and kept a three-gallon pot of chili or stew going for hungry actor friends. He added to it every day, which improved it, he remembers.

And caviar and vodka is a favorite; he tells me there is American caviar to be had in South Carolina. Although not the same as Russian or Iranian, it is still very good, he claims.

Freshly caught swordfish has no equal, Cliff believes. His family dines on it often during their East Hampton summers. Broiled, smoked, or any way you cook it, it is a delicacy.

Cliff gave me his recipe for mussels (he calls them by the French *moules*) very reluctantly because, he says, it is a relatively undiscovered food in America and "if we give them too much publicity everyone will be demanding them up and down the eastern seaboard, and the price will increase drastically —witness the popularity of the clam in recent years." And mussels are tenderer, he adds.

MUSSELS (Moules)

From Cliff Robertson

4 dozen fresh mussels	1 clove garlic, finely minced
½ cup dry white wine (e.g.,	(optional)
chablis)	½ cup milk
2 tablespoons cold water	½ cup cream
2 or 3 scallions, finely chopped	¼ cup chablis
2 stalks celery, chopped	

Scrub the mussels, then soak in cold water about 20 minutes to dislodge sand. If you wish, put 1 tablespoon dry mustard in the water which causes the mussels to spit out the sand.

Put mussels in a large pot with cover in the ½ cup wine and the water and steam them until shells open (3–5 minutes). Drain and reserve broth.

Lightly sauté scallions, celery, and garlic. Add and heat, but don't boil, milk, cream, ¼ cup chablis, and the wine broth. Add mussels to the milky broth and stir. The meat can be taken from the shells with a small fork and dipped in the broth; then drink the broth.

Fit for a rajah, says Cliff.   SERVES 4

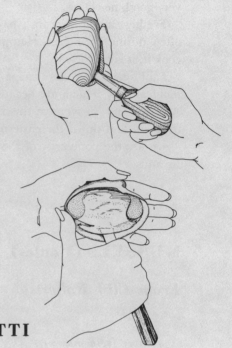

CLAM SAUCE FOR SPAGHETTI

From Cliff Robertson

2 cups chopped clams
Clam juice
4 teaspoons very finely chopped
  garlic
3 tablespoons finely chopped celery
2 tablespoons chopped fresh parsley

3 tablespoons finely chopped
  scallions
Butter and olive oil
⅓ cup chablis or other dry white
  wine
Salt and pepper to taste

If using fresh clams, open 18–24 (they are easier to open if they are well chilled in the refrigerator), remove the clams, and reserve the juice. Chop the clams somewhat coarsely.

Sauté very slowly garlic, celery, scallions, and parsley in butter or half butter, half olive oil. When these vegetables are a little soft, add chablis, clams, juice, salt, and pepper. Cook for 2 or 3 minutes until the clams are hot.

Serve over spaghetti or any thin pasta which has been cooked until firm, not mushy or sticky.   SERVES 4

Clams can be opened by steaming until the heat forces the shells open, or by chilling them several hours in the refrigerator, then knifing them open.

Steaming (from Joe Hyde's cookbook *Love, Thyme and Butter*):

"Scrub the clams with a stiff brush under cold running water. Place them in a deep roasting pan and put in oven (preheated to 400° for 20 minutes, or until all the clams open. Remove from oven and extract the clam meat from the shell. Pour the juice from the clams into a bowl. Rinse the clams in the juice to remove any sand—simply stir them around in the juice and remove to a strainer. Let the sand settle to the bottom of the bowl of juice and carefully pour off the juice, saving it for the chowder."

Opening chilled clams (from *Craig Claiborne's Favorites*, Vol. 2, Quadrangle):

"For the nonexpert and would-be clam shucker there are two things to remember that enormously facilitate opening the bivalves. Clams are closed tightly because of the powerful (but delicious and tender) muscle that joins the two shells and keeps the shells well-seated. If the clams are well-chilled before they are to be opened, the muscle tends to relax. The clams can be chilled for several hours in the refrigerator or briefly (without freezing) in the freezer. It is also imperative that the clam knife be sharp to facilitate its insertion between the 'jaws' of the clam. Avoid those guillotinelike clam-shucking gadgets. They mangle clams and are quite frankly an abomination."

Chapter 4

VEGETABLES

BIRCH BAYH

Senator from Indiana

As a young man, Senator Birch Bayh was interested in farming (he won a 4-H tomato growing championship), boxing, baseball, and debating.

After two years in the Army and graduation from Purdue, Senator Bayh married and settled on a large Indiana farm. His career as a farmer was short-lived, however, as he became involved in state politics and served in Indiana's legislature. This led him to law school, a period of practicing law, and the determination to take Homer Capehart's seat in the United States Senate. He has been an effective Democratic liberal Senator since 1962 and had one brief but unsuccessful try at the presidency in 1976.

As a well-known and well-traveled national figure, he receives invitations to beautifully executed social occasions and partakes of the finest of foods and wines. But they hold no temptation for him, as he has little interest in food. "Green beans, cooked any way" is his favorite dish, and here is a bean casserole the Bayhs enjoy.

GREEN BEAN CASSEROLE

From Senator Bayh

2 10-ounce packages frozen French-style green beans or 2 cans No. 303 French-style sliced green beans

1 10-ounce can mushroom soup
Grated Parmesan cheese
Slivered almonds

If beans are frozen, cook in ½ cup salted water until tender, then drain. Butter a casserole and make 2 layers—first beans, then soup, then cheese, and repeat. Scatter almonds over top. Bake 30 minutes in a preheated 350° oven.   SERVES 6

FRIED ZUCCHINI FLOWERS (Courgette en Beignet)

From Sans Souci Restaurant

Zucchini flowers (a few handfuls)
  (see note)
1 cup flour
½ teaspoon salt

1 egg, beaten
1 tablespoon melted butter
1 cup milk (or ½ cup beer and ½
  cup water for lighter batter)

Wash zucchini flowers and dry carefully. Make a batter of remaining ingredients. Dip flowers into batter and fry 1 or 2 minutes in mild oil (safflower or corn oil is good).   SERVES 4

AUTHOR'S NOTE: Pick zucchini flowers before they form themselves into the slim vegetable.

FRIED ZUCCHINI STRIPS

From Sans Souci Restaurant

This is a Mediterranean dish, but not a well-known one. Cut ends from a zucchini squash. Cut into long ½-inch-thick strips and dip into batter for Fried Zucchini Flowers and fry. Just a few minutes' frying time is enough, as the batter should be crisp and the vegetable just a little underdone.
    Serve as a vegetable or hot appetizer.   SERVES 2

MAURITIAN LENTILS (Dholl)

From the home of Ambassador Keeley

1 pound lentils (the small, grayish
  Indian ones if possible)
1 tablespoon oil
1 onion, chopped
1 clove garlic, minced

1 inch ginger root, crushed
1 tablespoon chopped fresh thyme or
  1 teaspoon dried
1 tablespoon chopped fresh parsley
Salt to taste

Soak lentils 3 hours. Wash well. Cover with water 3 inches above lentils and boil until water is absorbed. Lentils should become a purée; if not, add more water.

In another pan heat oil with onion, garlic, ginger, thyme, and parsley. Add to lentils. Add salt to taste. Serve hot with Mauritian Fish (Vinday), page 116 and Mauritian Chutney (Cotomili), page 199.   SERVES 6–8

SAM NUNN

Senator from Georgia

Sam Nunn, a conservative Democrat, is the great-nephew of Georgia's late legendary Senator Carl Vinson.

An Emory Law School graduate, he entered state politics and, in 1972, national politics to become, at age thirty-four, the second youngest senator in that select group.

He is six feet tall, athletic, and jogs as often as possible. He startled his American colleagues and his Chinese hosts when he recently traveled to China on a fact-finding trip and insisted on rising early each day to jog in the Peking parks.

The Nunns like simple and nutritious food and recommend their Sweet and Sour Baked Beans.

"Sweet and Sour Baked Beans is an old family recipe used originally for Fourth of July; however, my wife, Colleen, prepares this dish frequently for informal entertaining."

SWEET AND SOUR BAKED BEANS

From Senator Nunn

4 large onions, cut in rings
½–1 cup brown sugar (see note)
1 teaspoon dry mustard
1 teaspoon garlic powder
1 teaspoon salt
½ cup cider vinegar
15 ounces dried lima beans, cooked
according to package directions

1 16-ounce can green lima beans,
drained
1 16-ounce can dark red kidney
beans, drained
1 16-ounce can New England style
baked beans, drained
8 slices bacon, cooked, drained, and
crumbled

Place onions in skillet. Add sugar, mustard, garlic powder, salt, and vinegar. Cook 20 minutes covered. Add onion mixture to beans. Add crumbled bacon. Pour into 3-quart casserole and bake in a preheated 350° oven for 1 hour.

SERVES 6–8

AUTHOR'S NOTE: One cup sugar is ½ too much, unless you like very sweet beans.

SQUAW CORN

From Warren Weaver, Jr.

2 slices thick bacon
½ cup chopped onion
½ cup chopped green pepper
1 8-ounce can cream-style corn
2 eggs

½ cup cubed sharp cheese
(optional)
1 tomato, peeled, seeded, and diced
(optional)

Cut bacon into small squares and fry in a skillet until nearly done. When enough fat has accumulated, add onion and green pepper and cook over medium heat until tender. Add corn and cook a few minutes, stirring gently. Add eggs 1 at a time, stirring until the mixture thickens. Just before the eggs reach the scrambled consistency preferred by the cook, add cheese and tomato, making sure the latter has been thoroughly drained. Heat through and serve.

SERVES 4

JACOB JAVITS

Senator from New York

Senator Jacob Javits has been New York's Republican liberal senator for more than twenty years. His youth was spent in hard work in New York's garment industry; as janitor of tenement houses; and in years of study earning a law degree, supporting himself at the same time. He remembers an inexpensive but delicious dish from childhood called *prokas,* which is cabbage leaves stuffed with beef and covered with sauce.

The word "prokas" was researched in a dozen cookbooks and dictionaries, both American and foreign, and could not be found, and so I asked Senator Javits about it. He believes the word to be Hungarian. The senator's father was born in Russia, he said, and in 1913 when he was nine years old, the parents threw his father across the border into what was then Austro-Hungary. Thus, the Hungarian influence in their cooking.

STUFFED CABBAGE ("Prokas")

From Senator Javits

1 head cabbage
1 pound ground chuck
1 cup cooked rice
½ teaspoon salt
Worcestershire sauce to taste
Garlic powder to taste
2 onions, sliced

1½–2 tablespoons sweet Hungarian
   paprika or 1½ teaspoons
   American paprika
1 28-ounce can tomato purée
2 tablespoons brown sugar
2 tablespoons granulated sugar
Juice of 1 lemon

Separate cabbage leaves by pouring boiling water over and let sit until soft. Drain off water and separate leaves.

Mix meat with cooked rice, salt, Worcestershire, and garlic powder. Place 1 tablespoon of this mixture in each cabbage leaf; roll and fasten with toothpick.

Brown onions in bottom of pot, adding paprika. Put cabbage rolls on top of onions. Add tomato purée, sugars, and lemon juice to cover and cook on slow flame for 1 or 1½ hours, adding water as needed, or put in a preheated 350° oven for same time, adding water.   SERVES 6

AUTHOR'S NOTE: Good served with blob of sour cream.

VEGETABLES

HOMEMADE GERMAN NOODLES (Spätzle)

From Embassy of Germany

2¼ cups sifted flour
1 egg, beaten
⅔ cup water

½ teaspoon salt
¼ cup melted butter
¼ cup sour cream (optional)

Mix flour, egg, water, and salt. If the egg is large, use a little less water to make a soft dough that will not flow and is stiff enough so that it will not run off a spoon. Let the batter stand for 30 minutes. Scoop up some of the batter and place on a cutting board.

With a sharp knife (dip knife in flour occasionally to keep from becoming sticky) cut off *very thin* slices of the dough and drop the pieces directly from the board into a large kettle of boiling salted water. The spätzle should be about ¼ inch thick and less than 1 inch long. They will rise to the surface when they are cooked. Drain them well in a colander and transfer them to a deep, heated serving dish.

Pour melted butter over them and, if desired, stir in the warmed sour cream. Shake the spätzel well in the cream and butter before serving.   SERVES 6

BACON-WRAPPED BEANS

From Representative Montgomery

2 1-pound cans whole green beans
Bacon
Italian dressing

Italian seasoning
2 beef bouillon cubes

Bunch 6–8 beans and wrap with bacon. Secure with toothpick. Continue until all beans are used. Place in a casserole and drizzle some liquid Italian dressing over all, but do not smother. Sprinkle with Italian seasoning. Crush bouillon cubes and sprinkle over beans. Let stand for several hours or overnight. Bake in a preheated 350° oven for 40 minutes or until bacon is cooked.   SERVES 6

AUTHOR'S NOTE: This is not an unusual dish, but it has the advantage of (1) being done ahead of time and (2) not having a "canned" taste—thanks to the marinade.

CORN PUDDING

From Representative Montgomery

1 10-ounce package frozen cream-
   style corn (canned cream corn
   may be substituted)

2 eggs, well beaten
3 tablespoons butter, melted
Salt and pepper to taste

Let corn thaw. Add milk, eggs, and butter. Place in greased 1–1½-quart casserole and bake in a preheated 350° oven for 45–50 minutes.   SERVES 4 OR 5

FRIED ITALIAN PEPPERS

From Representative Rodino

12 long peppers (see note)
Olive oil for frying

Salt and pepper to taste
4 eggs, beaten

Wash, core, and cut peppers lengthwise. Fry in deep hot oil until golden tender. Drain the oil from the peppers and add beaten eggs with salt and pepper. Stir until eggs are cooked.

   This is also an excellent sandwich filling—a hot sandwich on good Italian or French bread.   SERVES 2

AUTHOR'S NOTE: The seed catalogue calls them "sweet banana peppers," but just be sure you use sweet, not hot, peppers.

FRIED ZUCCHINI

From Representative Rodino

4 zucchini squash
1 clove garlic, minced
1 teaspoon dried oregano

Salt and pepper to taste
½ cup olive oil

Wash and cut zucchini into rounds. Add garlic, oregano, salt, and pepper and fry in hot oil. Drain and serve.   SERVES 6

CARL BERNSTEIN

Journalist

Carl Bernstein, a native Washingtonian, is only thirty-four years old, but his accomplishments are awesome: eight years' experience on daily newspapers, including six years on the Washington *Post*, several journalism awards, including the Pulitzer (1973), two best sellers, *All the President's Men* and *The Final Days*, written with Robert Woodward.

To his credit, or discredit, depending on your politics, he was to an inestimable degree responsible for bringing to ouster and disgrace a two-term President of the United States.

Carl is not tall and not heavy and wears his thick hair, mostly black but now with gray appearing, in a long, somewhat unkempt style. He resigned from the Washington *Post* in 1976 and spends his time in New York and Washington with his wife, Nora Ephron, an author and associate editor of *Esquire* magazine. He is working on a book about political witch hunts.

They both like to cook, and they are both adept at it. Nora's recipe for borscht, a beautiful borscht, is on page 23. Carl's recipe for Spaghetti alla Cecca follows.

SPAGHETTI WITH BASIL AND TOMATO SAUCE (Spaghetti alla Cecca)

From Carl Bernstein

6 large summer tomatoes
1½ cups fresh basil
⅓–¾ cups olive oil

Salt and pepper to taste
1 pound spaghetti

Cut tomatoes in thin wedges and put in a large bowl with basil, oil, salt, and pepper. Let it sit for 3 or 4 hours.

Cook spaghetti al dente, drain, and toss with tomato mixture.

Says Carl: "This is an extraordinary combination—hot pasta and cold tomatoes—light and delicate as a salad."   SERVES 6

EGGPLANT CASSEROLE

From the home of President Carter

1 large eggplant, peeled	*2 cups peeled, chopped tomatoes*
1 teaspoon salt	*Pinch thyme*
Pepper to taste	*¼ cup chopped fresh parsley*
3 tablespoons butter	*Salt and pepper to taste*
3 tablespoons salad oil	*½ cup bread crumbs*
1 cup chopped onion	*½ cup grated Gruyère or mozzarella*
2 cloves garlic, minced	*cheese (see note)*

Slice eggplant into 8 1-inch-thick slices. Trim so they are approximately the same size. Save trimmings. Place slices in lightly oiled glass baking dish. Sprinkle with salt and pepper. Broil 5 minutes or until lightly browned on 1 side.

Heat oil and butter in saucepan. Add onion and garlic and cook 7–10 minutes, until onion is soft. Add tomatoes and diced eggplant trimmings and simmer until thick, 12–15 minutes. Add thyme, parsley, salt and pepper to taste, and bread crumbs.

Turn unbroiled side of eggplant up and spoon tomato mixture over the eggplant. Sprinkle with cheese and bake in a preheated 350° oven for 25–30 minutes or until tender.   SERVES 4

AUTHOR'S NOTE: I think *1 cup or more* cheese makes the dish more delicious.

GARLIC GRITS

From Senator Talmadge

1 cup grits (quick-cooking or non-	*1½ tablespoon Worcestershire sauce*
quick may be used)	*Dash Tabasco sauce*
4 tablespoons butter	*1 clove garlic, mashed*
¾ pound sharp cheese, grated	*3 or 4 egg whites, stiffly beaten*
3 egg yolks, mixed with small	
amount of cream	

Cook grits as usual. When cooked, stir in butter, all but 3 tablespoons cheese, egg yolks, Worcestershire, Tabasco, and garlic. Cool this mixture. Fold in egg whites. Sprinkle remaining grated cheese on top. Bake in a preheated 400° oven for ½ hour or until browned a bit.   SERVES 6

CHEESE GRITS

From David Eisenhower

1 cup quick-cooking grits
4 tablespoons margarine
⅔ cup grated longhorn cheese
⅔ cup grated sharp Cheddar cheese

1 egg, beaten
1 teaspoon salt
Dash Tabasco sauce
Paprika

Cook grits according to manufacturer's direction until thickened. Turn off heat. Add margarine, cheeses, egg, salt, and Tabasco. Stir thoroughly. Pour into buttered casserole. Bake in a preheated 300° oven for 1 hour. Sprinkle with paprika before serving.   SERVES 6

AUTHOR'S NOTE: For my taste a few dashes of Tabasco are nice, since grits and cheese are somewhat bland; also I think 30–45 minutes is plenty of oven time, since grits are already cooked and only cheese must melt and permeate.

RED CABBAGE WITH APPLE AND ONION

From Embassy of Germany

1 medium onion, diced
2 tablespoons bacon fat
1 apple, diced
1 small head red cabbage
1 cup boiling water

1 tablespoon brown sugar
1½ teaspoons salt
Pinch pepper
2 tablespoons vinegar

Sauté onion in bacon fat. Add apple. Shred cabbage and put in pot with onion and apple. Add boiling water and cook about 30 minutes or until cabbage is tender. Combine brown sugar, salt, pepper, and vinegar and stir into cabbage. Heat thoroughly and serve. If you prefer a more tart dish, add a little more vinegar.   SERVES 4

LAWTON CHILES

Senator from Florida

Florida sent lawyer Lawton Chiles, forty-seven, to the Senate in 1971. Like his Senate colleague Dick Clark of Iowa, he credits his election to the fact that he walked 1,000 miles across Florida and talked to 40,000 persons.

The six-foot 175-pound senator likes to hunt and fish, jog, and play football. He also likes delicious fried corn.

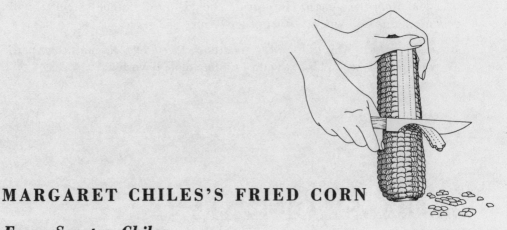

MARGARET CHILES'S FRIED CORN

From Senator Chiles

6 slices bacon
10 ears fresh corn
Milk

3 tablespoons butter
Salt and pepper to taste

Fry bacon, drain, crumble, and set aside, leaving fat from bacon in skillet.

Prepare corn in the following manner: Hold ear perpendicular to cutting board. With sharp knife, slice downward, cutting off tip ends of kernels—then scrape milk out of remaining part of kernels.

Heat bacon fat in skillet and add scraped corn and kernel tips. Fry lightly for 3 minutes, stirring constantly. Add enough milk to make creamed corn consistency. Add butter. Cook another 5 minutes. Add salt and pepper. Pour in serving dish and sprinkle crushed bacon over all.   SERVES 6

SQUASH WITH DILL (Tok Fovelek)

From Antal Dorati

4 or 5 yellow summer squash
Salt
1½ medium onions, finely chopped
¼ cup chopped fresh dill or 2
   teaspoons dried

2 or 3 tablespoons bacon drippings
1–2 teaspoons vinegar
2 cups sour cream

Peel yellow squash and slice into long strips with vegetable peeler. Salt the raw vegetable and leave to drain in colander for ½ hour or so. Press with hands or wooden spoon until the brine is squeezed out.

Meanwhile, sauté onions and dill lightly in bacon drippings. Add the squash. Cover and simmer gently 5 or 10 minutes, until the squash is tender. The natural liquid from the squash will provide enough juice, but be careful the dish does not burn. Add vinegar, stir in sour cream, and serve.   SERVES 6

AUTHOR'S NOTE: This dish is very good hot and equally delicious cold, particularly in spring when dill is fresh and therefore more flavorful.

EMBASSY OF ITALY

Washington, D.C.

The ambassador from Italy, Roberto Gaja, is in his sixties and has three grown children. He is aesthetic, intellectual, likes music, the arts, and politics, but has little interest in eating and practically none in cooking. His predecessor, Ambassador Egidio Ortona, was what Americans like to think of as typically Italian—gregarious, charming, and as one could see at a glance, very interested in the art of dining.

A typical Italian dinner served at the Italian Embassy begins with antipasto. Several suggestions for this first course are: prosciutto (Italian ham) slices rolled around bread sticks, which can be bought in any good food store, on the gourmet shelf of most supermarkets, or freshly made at Italian bakeries; rolled prosciutto slices served beside wedges of chilled melon; prosciutto with chilled figs; pieces of cheese to be eaten with wedges of pears—which brings to mind an old Italian saying: "Never tell a countryman [farmer] how good is cheese and pears because you will never again get any more cheese and pears."

Next is the pasta or rice course followed by the main course, which is meat or fish, then fruit and dessert, and, of course, espresso, and all washed down with good Italian wine. Cheese is usually served only for luncheon, as Italian cheeses are somewhat rich and heavy and not appropriate for dinner at the embassy.

Rice is a daily necessity for Italians from the northern part of Italy—just as pasta is the main staple for the rest of Italy. But it is neglected in the United States. We should take the extra effort to cook rice the way the Italians do, that is, slowly, stirring often, adding a glassful of wine, and cooking it always in broth, not water. The Venetians add a large chunk of butter to the rice at the last minute, but no cooking must take place after the butter is added.

We list in this section several recipes, not on pasta, but rice, as it has been more neglected than the pasta family.

SAFFRON RICE (Risotto Saffron)

From Embassy of Italy

2 thin slices onion
1 tablespoon olive oil
5 tablespoons butter
2 cups long-grain rice (it is interesting that the Italian donor of this recipe said that Uncle Ben's is used by many in Italy)

4 cups hot chicken broth (or water if you wish)
½ cup marsala or chablis
¾ teaspoon (approximately) powdered saffron
1½ cups grated Parmesan cheese

Sauté onion gently in oil and 1 tablespoon of the butter until soft. Add the rice. Add some of the broth (which may be made with bouillon cubes if you do not have homemade stock on hand). Stir while slowly adding the liquid. Liquid should disappear with the stirring; then add more. Stir frequently while cooking for about 20 minutes. The rice will be creamy and somewhat sticky, but this is as it should be.

Pour wine into the rice and add saffron, which has been dissolved in 3 tablespoons of the broth. The rice can cook 5 or 10 minutes more until it is tender.

Remove from fire and with a long 2-pronged fork (not spoon, as it mashes the rice to a mush), stir in cheese and the remaining 4 tablespoons butter. Cover for 3 or 4 minutes and serve.   SERVES 8–10

AUTHOR'S NOTE: Rice will be a bit less gummy if you use short- or medium-grain rice, not long-grain.

RICE WITH LAMB

From Embassy of Italy

Use method of cooking rice as described in Saffron Rice, with basic ingredients:
1 cup rice to 2 cups broth or water.

Soften 2 chopped onions in butter, stir in 1 pound cubed lamb. When the meat is a little brown, add 2 large fresh chopped tomatoes (or 1 small can tomatoes, chopped), salt, pepper, and some of the chicken stock. Cover and simmer until meat is nearly cooked. Add rice and rest of broth, which should be hot, and cook until rice is done.   SERVES 4

RICE WITH VEAL LIVER

From Embassy of Italy

Use method of cooking rice as described in Saffron Rice, with basic ingredients:
1 cup rice to 2 cups broth or water.

Sauté 1 pound thin slices of veal liver with chunks of onion in a mixture of butter and olive oil for 5 or 10 minutes. Do not overcook the liver. Add ¼ cup white wine, salt, and pepper. Add rice and broth and cook until tender.

                                                                          SERVES 4

RICE WITH SAUSAGE

From Embassy of Italy

1 pound mild Italian sausage   *1 cup rice*
2 onions, coarsely chopped   *4 tablespoons butter*
2 cups boiling water or broth   *¾ cup grated Parmesan cheese*

Peel sausage, cut in chunks, and sauté with onions. There will be much fat from meat; discard some. Add water or broth and cook 5 minutes, then add rice and cook about 25 minutes, stirring frequently.

When the rice is cooked, add butter and cheese before serving.   SERVES 4

JOHN TUNNEY

Senator from California

John Varick Tunney and his siblings never knew their father as one-time world heavyweight boxing champion (Jack Dempsey's opponent in the famous fight). They knew him instead as a millionaire businessman, and John grew up with money and privilege.

John Tunney was graduated from Yale and took an interest in politics at the University of Virginia, where he earned a law degree. There, he was roommate of Senator Edward Kennedy and helped Ted campaign for John F. Kennedy's presidency.

Senator Tunney was an air force lawyer, worked on Wall Street, and practiced law in California before trying for Congress. He served six years in the U. S. House of Representatives and six in the Senate.

Senator Tunney is 6'3", athletic in build at 190 pounds, and plays well a half-dozen sports including golf, tennis, skiing, and sailing. He is fond of spicy food and recommends an Indonesian specialty, Nasi Goreng, which, he points out, is the main part of a very elaborate meal called Rice Table.

INDONESIAN RICE (Nasi Goreng)

From Senator Tunney

1 large onion, finely chopped
Oil for sautéing
1 tablespoon Sambal Oelek (see note)
1½ pounds round steak, pork loin, or stew meat (cut in bite-sized pieces)

Salt to taste
2 cups cooked rice (preferably cooked the day before)

Sauté onion in oil until transparent; don't brown. Add Sambal Oelek and stir. Then add the meat and salt. Fry, stirring, until meat is tender, about 20 minutes. Mix with rice and more salt. Serve immediately.   SERVES 4

Side dishes to accompany Nasi Goreng: celery, carrots, radishes, fried bananas, and/or tossed green salad.

AUTHOR'S NOTE: Sambal Oelek, which is used in most Indonesian meals, is a very hot seasoning and should be used with caution until one is familiar with it.

ARMENIAN RICE

From Warren Weaver, Jr.

4 tablespoons butter
1 pound chicken livers
2 tablespoons (or more) chopped
    onion
2 teaspoons finely chopped garlic
½ cup mushrooms, sliced or diced
1 green pepper, shredded

¼ teaspoon (or more) chili pepper
½ teaspoon dry mustard
2½ cups rice
2 tablespoons beef bouillon base
2 tablespoons tomato paste
5 cups beef broth

Melt butter in skillet and brown chicken livers moderately well. Remove livers, slice thick, and reserve. Add onion and garlic and cook for 1 minute. Add mushrooms, green pepper, chili pepper, and dry mustard and cook for 2 minutes. Add rice (you may need more butter to coat the mixture) and cook about 3 minutes, stirring. Add bouillon base and tomato paste, stirring to blend. Add broth to cover, cover skillet, and simmer until rice is tender but not overdone, 20 minutes or so. About ½ the broth should be added in 2 or more installments during the simmering. When done, put rice mixture into a large casserole and keep warm in a 200° oven.

1 eggplant, unskinned and sliced
Cooking oil
½ cup (or more) whole almonds
2 apples, cored, skinned, and sliced
Butter
2 large onions, thickly sliced

3 tomatoes, thickly sliced
1 green pepper, shredded
2 tablespoons (or more) peach
    preserves
8 slices fried bacon, crumbled

Fry eggplant until golden in hot oil, then almonds in same skillet until nicely brown (careful). Brown apple slices in butter, then onions until dark. Add all these plus tomatoes, green pepper (raw), peach preserves, and reserved chicken livers to rice, stirring carefully to mix. Serve rice hot, garnished with bacon.

SERVES 8

BEXAR COUNTY (TEXAS) BEAN CASSEROLE

From Ambassador Shannon

½ cup chopped onion
2 tablespoons bacon drippings
½ cup chopped celery
½ cup sliced mushrooms
2 cups canned tomatoes
2 tablespoons brown sugar
1 teaspoon salt

1 teaspoon pepper
2 tablespoons chopped fresh parsley
2 cloves garlic, mashed
Dash Tabasco
2 pounds fresh or frozen string beans
1 cup grated Cheddar cheese
1 cup bread crumbs

Sauté onion in bacon drippings in large skillet. Add remaining ingredients except beans, cheese, and bread crumbs. Simmer for 30 minutes, stirring often.

Put cooked green beans in buttered casserole in alternate layers with sauce and grated cheese. Top with bread crumbs and bake in a preheated 325° oven for 30 minutes.   SERVES 8

OKRA AND TOMATO

From the home of Senator Johnston

½ pound fresh okra or 2 10-ounce
  packages frozen
1 medium onion, chopped
2 cloves garlic, minced
6 fresh tomatoes, coarsely chopped,
  or 1 1-pound 10-ounce can
  stewed tomatoes

3 tablespoons Worcestershire sauce
Seasoned bread crumbs

This is an exquisite creole combination, particularly if the vegetables are fresh.

If fresh, wash okra, chop off the tops, and cut into small pieces (½-inch rings or smaller). Sauté with onion and garlic until the mixture loses some of its "gooeyness." Add tomatoes and Worcestershire and put in a buttered casserole, bread crumbs on top, and cook in a preheated 350° oven for ½ hour.

                                                                SERVES 4–6

FRANK IKARD

Director of the American Petroleum Institute

Frank and Jane Ikard are both in their second marriages and they share cooking as a common and consuming hobby. Mrs. Ikard is Jayne Brumley, a former correspondent for *Newsweek,* and Frank is a former congressman from Texas. He now holds the most interesting job in Washington and one of the most powerful—head of the oil lobby.

They do most of their entertaining at their West Virginia farm near Shepherdstown on the Potomac River. The 300-acre farm supports cattle and fruits and vegetables. The herb garden yields such unusuals as sweet woodruff, hissop, horseradish, and of course the standard basil, dill, tarragon, and other herbs.

One of the favorite menus for guests at the farm is chili, preferably made a day before. This is a highly spiced authentic Texas-near-Mexican-border chili. When Mrs. Ikard has her way, she serves her New England oyster stew with her husband's Texas jalapeño corn bread.

Puréed Turnips, made with Cheddar cheese, is a favorite. The Ikards enjoy playing a joke on their friends with this one by asking, "Do you like turnips?" The answer is usually negative. Then after three helpings of this dish they reveal the casserole's identity.

PURÉED TURNIPS

From Frank Ikard

3 cups cooked mashed turnips
1 onion, finely chopped
2 tablespoons butter
Salt and pepper to taste

¾ teaspoon sugar
1 egg, beaten
½ cup grated Cheddar cheese
Paprika

Boil turnips until tender and drain in colander.

Sauté onion in butter. Add it and salt and pepper to turnips. Add sugar, egg, and cheese. Mix and mash. Put in baking dish and sprinkle with paprika. Bake in a preheated 350° oven for 15 minutes.   SERVES 6

BLACK-EYED PEAS WITH HOG JOWL

From Representative Montgomery

1 pound dried black-eyed peas
1/4 pound smoked hog jowl
1 clove garlic, mashed

1/2 pod red pepper, minced
Salt to taste

Place peas in a heavy pot (enameled or stainless steel), cover with cold water, and soak overnight. Drain off water and add remaining ingredients. Add water to cover and bring to boil. Reduce heat to simmer and cook until peas are tender, which will take several hours.　　　　　SERVES 6

Sonny's charming and gracious mother, Emily Tims, told me: "These are traditional for New Year's Day, served with corn bread and ham. Mighty good eating!"

GREEN SPAGHETTI (Spaghetti Verde)

From the home of Senator Moynihan

1/2 cup finely puréed spinach
1 egg
1 tablespoon vegetable oil

1/4 teaspoon coarse salt (use kosher salt)
2 cups flour

Squeeze dry the spinach and gradually add egg, oil, salt, and flour, stirring and mixing until the mixture is smooth. Cover dough and set aside for 30 minutes.

If you have a pasta machine, make spaghetti; if not, roll the dough thin (to avoid drying out the dough, gently fold up after rolling). When finished, form a big log roll and cut in thin strips. Drop the noodles into boiling salted water for 4 minutes.　　　　　SERVES 5

PAN-FRIED POTATOES ROESTI

From Embassy of Switzerland

2 pounds potatoes   Cooking fat or clarified butter

Boil potatoes in their skins until they are a bit underdone. Peel and grate coarsely or cut into very thin slices. Heat the fat and put potatoes in frying pan. Cook slowly, not stirring, until a round crisp "cake" develops. Turn this "cake" over and brown it, then serve.   SERVES 6

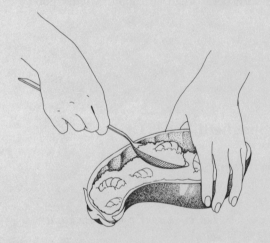

EGGPLANT STUFFED WITH SHRIMP

From the home of Senator Johnston

1 large eggplant   Salt and pepper to taste
1 medium onion, cut up   Seasoned bread crumbs
1 or 2 cloves garlic, finely minced
½–1 pound small shrimp (if large
    shrimp are used, cut them up)

Bake or boil eggplant, cut in half lengthwise, and scoop out the pulp. Mash. Sauté onion and garlic. Cook and peel shrimp. Add shrimp, onion, and garlic to the mashed eggplant. Put mixture back into eggplant shell, sprinkle bread crumbs over, and bake in a preheated 350° oven for 20 or 25 minutes. SERVES 2

EGGPLANT STUFFED WITH TOMATOES

From the home of Senator Johnston

1 large eggplant	*Worcestershire sauce*
3 or 4 fresh tomatoes	*Seasoned bread crumbs*
Parsley	

Cut up tomatoes and simmer with parsley and Worcestershire. Follow directions for Eggplant Stuffed with Shrimp (above), mixing instead the tomatoes with the mashed cooked eggplant, and put in oven, bread crumbs on top, for 20 or 25 minutes.   SERVES 2

STUFFED PEPPERS

From the home of Senator Griffin

4 large green peppers	*1 cup cooked rice*
3 tablespoons minced onion	*½ teaspoon salt*
2 tablespoons butter	*⅛ teaspoon paprika*
½ pound ground beef	*¼ teaspoon Worcestershire sauce*

Prepare pepper cases by cutting stem ends from peppers. Remove seeds and veins. Drop peppers into boiling salted water and cook uncovered until they are nearly tender, about 5 minutes. Drain well.

Sauté onion in butter, add ground meat, and cook until meat loses red color. Mix rice with salt, paprika, and Worcestershire.

Stuff the peppers with mixture and place in a shallow pan with a small amount of water. Bake in a preheated 350° oven for 10–15 minutes.   SERVES 4

HOLSTEINER CHAMPIGNONS

From Embassy of Great Britain

¾ pound mushrooms, sliced
Butter for sautéing
2 tablespoons flour
1 cup milk
Salt to taste
Paprika to taste
3 tomatoes, peeled and sliced or 1½
   cups canned, somewhat drained

2 hard-boiled eggs, sliced
½ cup stewed celery or onions (or a
   mixture), stewed in as little water
   as possible
Dash sherry

Sauté mushrooms in butter for 4 minutes. Remove mushrooms. Add flour to the panful of juices. Make a smooth paste and slowly add milk to make a creamy sauce. Add seasonings and cook for 5–7 minutes, stirring constantly. Add mushrooms, tomatoes, eggs, and celery. Cook over hot water for 10–15 minutes. Just before serving, add sherry.

This is good served with rice. SERVES 4–6

BRAISED ENDIVE

From the home of Ambassador Buchanan

6 medium endives (the firm conical-
   shaped Belgian endive)
2 tablespoons melted butter
1 teaspoon sugar

Salt to taste
Dash pepper
Chopped fresh parsley

Wash endives and put them in a heavy pot. Pour melted butter over them and sprinkle with sugar, salt, and pepper. Cover the dish and let it simmer gently for 15–20 minutes. It will make a liquid of its own. Uncover the dish for the last 5 minutes of cooking so that the color will become slightly golden. Sprinkle chopped parsley on top and serve. SERVES 4

VICHY CARROTS

From Stewart Richardson

4 bunches or packets carrots
3 tablespoons butter

3 teaspoons sugar

Peel carrots. Cut into 4-inch pieces. With peeler, round off cut edges. Place in cold water with butter and sugar. Cook for 18–20 minutes or until the carrots are fork-penetrable but not soft. May be held, covered, for 5–10 minutes with no heat.   SERVES 6

Chapter 5

EGGS AND CHEESE

JAMES RESTON

Columnist, the New York Times

Born in Clydebank, Scotland, in 1909, the nickname is rightfully earned. James "Scotty" Reston has been with the New York *Times* for nearly forty years as reporter, columnist, and vice-president and board member. He has been married for forty years and has three sons.

Although Scotty Reston exercises immense power at the New York *Times,* he is a pipe and slippers kind of man and he likes to write in comfort in his Cleveland Park Washington home.

He likes to cook breakfast, usually omelet with cheese or onion, and "I use up half of Texas' grapefruit crop in the winter by squeezing one or two daily for the breakfast juice." Sometimes he prepares what he calls Eggs Fulton, named for Judge Fulton of Illinois, who was Sally Reston's father.

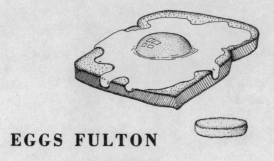

EGGS FULTON

From James Reston

The French make a similar dish, naming it *pain perdu* (lost bread.)

Use a slice of white bread from which a round hole has been cut with a doughnut or cookie cutter. Butter the bread generously on both sides, fry for 1 minute on each side, and when it is slightly toasty, break an egg into the hole and cook until the egg is firm, as any fried egg. Toast the rounds that were cut from the slice and serve them with Eggs Fulton.   SERVES 1

EGGS SARDOU

From the home of Tom Wicker

1 cup creamed spinach, piping hot   *2 eggs, poached*
2 artichoke bottoms, cooked   *¾ cup hollandaise sauce*

Make a base of spinach on serving plate, place artichoke cups on top. Put an egg in each and top with hollandaise.   SERVES 1

Pam Hill Wicker says: "This is one of those recipes which look deceptively simple. But if you're serving brunch, get up at eight; it takes a long time. I cook the artichokes whole, in boiling water, forty-five minutes, with a piece of lemon tied to the bottom. Then save the leaves for later use, and cut out the bottoms to use here."

It can be prepared with frozen creamed spinach, but always use freshly ground nutmeg, butter, a little cream, plus salt and pepper.

Recipes for hollandaise sauce appear on pages 197 and 198.

ROBERT KEELEY

U. S. Ambassador

Diplomat Robert Keeley and his wife, Louise, plunge enthusiastically into a new foreign assignment no matter what country is assigned. They learn the language (Bob speaks and reads Greek, French, and Arabic) and make good, usually lifetime, friends among the country's citizens. They set about understanding the people, politics, and customs with unusual insight.

Louise Keeley is well informed on both United States and world affairs. She assumes the traditional "wife's role" in the diplomatic service—entertaining with ease—with such enthusiasm that she could be an ambassador herself.

Bob Keeley is a true "foreign service brat." He was born in Lebanon and his father ultimately became ambassador to Greece. Bob became that embassy's political officer in Athens in 1966, then served in Jordan, Cambodia, and several African countries, and in the summer of 1976 became ambassador to Mauritius.

Through the State Department he has attended several language schools, was a fellow at the National Institute of Public Affairs, Stanford University, and a Woodrow Wilson Fellow at Princeton.

"I have no business being in your cookbook," Bob told me, "as I know nothing about cooking. True, I like to eat, do it regularly, prefer to eat well-prepared food, but am not wild about very exotic dishes."

"The only things I make at home that my family will eat are fried egg sandwiches and egg salad." The recipes are given here.

KEELEY'S EGG SALAD SANDWICHES

From Ambassador Keely

Finely chop hard-boiled eggs and celery. (Use the proportion of ¾ eggs to ¼ celery.) Add mayonnaise, prepared mustard, and horseradish to taste. Spread on soft white bread.

These sandwiches used to cost 15¢.

KEELEY'S FRIED EGG SANDWICHES

Melt a small pat of butter in frying pan, drop in raw egg, break yolk with spatula, spread yolk across all of white part of egg, and flip egg briefly when done on 1 side. Serve on plain white bread and smother with tomato ketchup. SERVES 1

BRUSSELS FONDUE (A Fried Cheese Entree)

From Ambassador Rush

4 tablespoons butter
5 tablespoons flour
1 cup cold milk
1 teaspoon salt
Pepper to taste
Grated nutmeg to taste
3 egg yolks
½ cup grated Gruyère cheese
Flour
1 egg, lightly beaten
Fresh bread crumbs

SAUCE:
1 pound tomatoes, cut up
1 onion, cut up
Salt and pepper to taste
1 bay leaf
Thyme to taste
1 cup water

Melt butter. Add 5 tablespoons flour and cook 3 minutes. Add milk and boil. Add salt, pepper, and nutmeg. Add egg yolks, 1 at a time, beating after each addition.

Bring to boil again. Add cheese. Remove to a bowl, cover with a buttered paper, and let cool. Beat once or twice while cooling to keep butter from separating. Refrigerate 5 or 6 hours. Make into small cakes about 1 inch thick and refrigerate until needed.

When ready to use, roll the cakes in flour, then in egg, then in fresh bread crumbs. Deep fry until puffed and golden, about 10 minutes, in very hot but not smoking oil. Remove and drain on a paper towel. Serve with tomato sauce.

SERVES 4

Sauce: Cook all sauce ingredients until tomatoes are soft and only 1 tablespoon of liquid remains. Strain through food mill.

NOTE: This same recipe may be used to make tiny round cheese balls served on toothpicks as appetizers at cocktail parties. Make ahead and reheat in very hot oven.

ARTHUR BURNS

Former Chairman of the Federal Reserve Board

Arthur Burns, former chairman of the Federal Reserve Board, is not an every-day cook, but when he is on vacation, usually summers in Vermont, Mrs. Burns sleeps late and her husband makes breakfast. He serves an artistic and attractive breakfast tray—much more creative than her version, says Mrs. Burns.

Chairman Burns is neat and orderly in the kitchen. He likes good, plain cooking like beef stew or pot roast. When he was head of the Reserve Board, he would come home from "The Fed" in the early evening and have a small glass of vodka, neat with no ice. He still does. He enjoys an hors d'oeuvre of smoked Nova Scotia salmon or chopped liver pâté.

His favorite dish to eat, not cook, is Mrs. Burns' Veal Piccata, page 55.

OMELET WITH HAM

From Arthur Burns

4 eggs
4 tablespoons milk
1 tablespoon butter

Handful cut-up pieces baked
Virginia ham

Have ready an omelet pan. (I use Mrs. Burns's old black iron crepe pan.) Beat eggs and milk hard and fast. Put butter in the pan and heat to sizzling.

Pour egg and milk mixture and ham pieces into the sizzling pan and cook omelet over high heat until the underside is golden. Turn the omelet over in the pan, let it sit a moment in the pan with little or no heat, and turn it out on a warm plate. Season at the table.   SERVES 2

EMBASSY OF FRANCE

Washington, D.C.

Madame Jacques Kosciusko-Morizet is taller than her husband, the ambassador, and very sure of herself. Standing in one of the grand reception rooms of the French Embassy Residence on Kalorama Road in Washington, she could be the ambassador, so imposing is she. Madame talked about the superiority of French food and dining.

When a French diplomat entertains an American in Washington, he feels it is ordinary courtesy to serve his guest French food, either in his home or in a good restaurant. Washington's finest dining rooms are French, and a typical choice would be Sans Souci (see pages 64–65 for commentary on this restaurant), Jean Pierre, Lion d'Or, or Bagatelle, all within walking distance of the White House.

The French Embassy is renowned for its well-organized, excellent kitchen staff, which has not changed substantially, though ambassadors come and go.

The Kosciusko-Morizets have recently returned to France and are replaced by Ambassador and Madame François de Laboulaye. Ambassador Laboulaye was born in Washington, D.C., and received his early schooling there; he later returned to the American Capital to attend Georgetown University.

The frosting on his career is the return to his birthplace as ambassador. He previously saw diplomatic service in Beirut, Ottawa, and was ambassador to Brazil and Japan.

Formal entertaining at the French Embassy is unsurpassed. In May 1976 President Ford was invited to a ceremonious state dinner with the President of France. The menu:

DINER

offert en l'honneur

de

SON EXCELLENCE
MONSIEUR LE PRÉSIDENT
DES ÉTATS-UNIS D'AMÉRIQUE

et de

MADAME GÉRALD FORD

par

MONSIEUR LE PRÉSIDENT
DE LA RÉPUBLIQUE FRANÇAISE

et

MADAME VALÉRY GISCARD D'ESTAING

Mardi 18 mai 1976

AMBASSADE DE FRANCE
Washington

Foie gras du Périgord
glacé à l'essence de truffes
Navarin de homard
aux légumes de printemps
Feuilleté de cailles aux raisins
Pommes moulées au jambon
Cœurs de laitues aux herbes
Fromages de France
Framboises glacées Élysée

Château d'Yquem 1971
Château Haut-Brion blanc 1970
Chambertin 1966 (Domaine Louis Latour)
Dom Pérignon 1969

CHILLED GOOSE LIVER PÂTÉ WITH TRUFFLES
(FROM PÉRIGORD REGION)
LOBSTER IN A STEW OF SPRING VEGETABLES
QUAIL WITH RAISINS IN PASTRY SHELL
POTATO NUGGETS WITH BITS OF HAM
HEARTS OF LETTUCE WITH HERBS
FRENCH CHEESES
CHILLED RASPBERRIES

The embassy recommends for American cooks some of its own preparations:
Quiche Lorraine, Cheese Soufflé, Chicken Marengo, Beef "à la Mode."

CHEESE SOUFFLÉ

From Embassy of France

⅓ cup butter
⅓ cup flour
3 cups milk
½ teaspoon salt

Pepper to taste
6 eggs, separated
1 cup grated Gruyère cheese

Melt butter in a saucepan. Blend flour into it. Slowly add milk, salt, and pepper and bring to a gentle boil, stirring with a whip or wooden spoon. Pull from heat and add egg yolks.

Beat egg whites and fold into the mixture. Add cheese.

Pour into a well-buttered, lightly floured soufflé mold. (If you do not have a soufflé mold, use an 8- or 9-inch pan or casserole which is 2 or 3 inches high. Also, fill it no more than ¾ full.) Bake in a preheated 420° oven for about 20 minutes. (Or try baking in a 375° oven for 25 or 30 minutes.) Serve at once as it will collapse. SERVES 4

QUICHE LORRAINE

From Embassy of France

Pastry for 1 8-inch pie shell
¾ cup diced cooked ham or bacon
½ cup grated Gruyère cheese
Freshly ground black pepper to taste

Nutmeg to taste
4 eggs, plus 3 egg yolks
1½ cups cream

Line an 8-inch pie pan with pastry (*pâte brise:* short pastry) and bake the pastry in a preheated 350° oven for 10 to 12 minutes without browning. Spread ham or bacon, cheese, pepper, and nutmeg on bottom of partially cooked pie shell.

Beat eggs slightly, add cream, and pour over the meat and cheese. Bake in 400° oven for 20 minutes. SERVES 6

AUTHOR'S NOTE: I think American ovens require longer baking time. The quiche will probably be "set" in 25 or 30 minutes.

TOMATO QUICHE

From the home of Robert Keeley .

½ cup minced onion
½ cup minced celery
½ cup minced green pepper
3 tablespoons butter
3 or 4 tomatoes, peeled and chopped
4 eggs, beaten
1 scant tablespoon sugar

1 cup grated Cheddar cheese or feta
Salt and pepper to taste
Fresh chopped herbs (parsley,
   tarragon, dill, basil in desired
   combination)
1 8-inch pie shell

Sauté onion, celery, and green pepper in butter. Add tomatoes and sauté until tomato juice is nearly absorbed. Cool slightly, then add eggs, sugar, cheese, salt, pepper, and herbs and pour into uncooked pie shell. Bake in a preheated 350° oven until crust is brown and quiche is "set," 45 minutes to 1 hour, usually.

This is delicious served hot or cold and can be frozen after it is baked. If frozen, reheat in 300° oven for 15–25 minutes until hot.   SERVES 6

AARON LATHAM

Journalist

Aaron Latham was senior editor for *New York* magazine until it was sold in 1976 and at thirty-three has held impressive jobs in the literary field. After graduating from Amherst College and earning a Ph.D. in English at Princeton, he worked for the Washington *Post* and went on to become an editor at *Esquire*. In addition to the lively copy he produced for *New York,* his first novel, *Orchids for Mother,* was published in May 1977.

When he is not in New York, he shares a beautiful Washington Watergate apartment with his wife, CBS correspondent Lesley Stahl. Their apartment on the fifteenth floor has oriental rugs and Helen Frankenthaler paintings and a terrace roof garden where they often entertain. The garden overlooks the Potomac River and the city's monuments, and for a Fourth of July supper, hamburgers and quiche Lorraine were served with the Capitol's fireworks for entertainment. Afterward sixteen of their guests came down from the roof and climbed on the oversize bed to watch a special Independence Day program with Walter Cronkite. Walter's mother was one of the viewers.

Aaron is comfortable in the role of cook. His parents taught him to do kitchen jobs along with his sister and she received guns and "boy's toys" at Christmas while a doll was usually included with his gifts.

Aaron, a Texan, wants to charcoal steak often, but defers to Lesley, who likes to prepare more complicated dishes, mostly French. Below we have a recipe from their kitchen.

BROCCOLI SOUFFLÉ

From Aaron Latham

3 tablespoons butter
3 tablespoons flour
1 cup milk
4 eggs, separated

Salt to taste
Prepared mustard to taste
Worcestershire sauce to taste
1 cup finely chopped broccoli

Melt butter in saucepan and stir in flour. Bring milk to a boil and pour into butter-flour mixture. Stir with a wire whisk until thick and smooth.

Beat in egg yolks 1 at a time. Add salt, mustard, and Worcestershire. Blend broccoli into mix. Beat egg whites and fold into the mixture. Pour into a 2-quart soufflé dish and bake in a preheated 375° oven for 30–40 minutes. Serve with hollandaise sauce.   SERVES 4

BREAD AND CHEESE CASSEROLE FROM THE PROVINCE OF VALAIS (Canton Valais)

From Embassy of Switzerland

1 loaf French bread, cut into 20 thin, firm slices	*1 quart milk*
	Nutmeg to taste
20 slices Emmenthal (Swiss) cheese	*Paprika to taste*
5 eggs	*Pepper to taste*

Alternate layers of bread and cheese in buttered ovenproof dish. Beat together eggs, milk, and spices and pour over layered casserole. Put dish in a pan of hot water, place in a preheated 350° oven and bake until golden brown and crusty.

SERVES 10

AUTHOR'S NOTE: If you use a shallow casserole dish that holds only 1 layer of bread and cheese, cook the dish 50 minutes to 1 hour. If your dish holds 2 layers of bread and cheese, you will need more time—about 1 hour 15 minutes.

PATRICK MOYNIHAN

Senator from New York

Senator Daniel Patrick Moynihan has served four successive Presidents of both parties in senior and cabinet-level positions. He has earned so many degrees, actual and honorary, and held so many important positions that his Who's Who reads like a testimonial. At age fifty he was elected senator from New York and is called the most colorful and charming Irishman since John F. Kennedy.

When in Cambridge Liz Moynihan entertained at the many informal gatherings of her husband's students. The lucky Harvard undergrads were treated to the specialty of the house—Lasagna Bolognese with homemade spinach lasagna noodles. "Pat is very fond of Italian food and we make pasta regularly." In deference to some of the students who were vegetarians, it became a popular dish when the Moynihans entertained.

Bouncy, exuberant 6'5" Pat Moynihan, like former Federal Reserve Chairman Arthur Burns, makes a good omelet. "It always turns out fluffy and perfect," he says. The recipe is on following page.

OMELETTE AUX FINES HERBES

From Senator Moynihan

3 eggs
¼ teaspoon salt
1 tablespoon cold water
2 tablespoons finely snipped fresh parsley
1 teaspoon finely snipped fresh tarragon

1 teaspoon finely snipped fresh marjoram
½ teaspoon finely snipped fresh thyme
1 teaspoon finely chopped shallots
1 tablespoon butter or margarine
1 sprig parsley

Combine eggs, salt, and water in a small bowl and beat, with rotary beater, until just combined, not frothy. Combine remaining ingredients except butter and parsley sprig. Stir into eggs, mixing well.

Slowly heat a medium-sized heavy skillet. (It is ready when a bit of cold water sprinkled over the surface sizzles and rolls off in drops.) Add butter or margarine and heat until it sizzles briskly (not browned). Quickly turn egg mixture into skillet and cook over medium-high heat. As omelet sets, loosen edge with spatula and tilt skillet, to let uncooked mixture run under set portion. When omelet is almost dry on top and golden brown on bottom, fold it over to edge of pan. Tilt out onto hot serving plate. Garnish with parsley sprig.

SERVES I OR 2

NOTE: If substituting dried herbs for fresh ones, use ½ the quantity.

JAMES VORENBERG

Professor, Harvard Law School

James Vorenberg graduated from Harvard University in 1948 and went on to learn the practical practice of law as a clerk to Supreme Court Justice Felix Frankfurter. He later became partner in a Boston law firm and a professor of law at Harvard. He also has held special assignments in Washington under various administrations. He served as director of President Johnson's Crime Commission and with the NAACP Legal Defense Fund, and he served with special prosecutor Archibald Cox until Cox was fired by President Nixon.

Harvard has a way of reclaiming its own, and Professor Vorenberg is in Cambridge again, teaching law and directing the Center for Criminal Justice.

For relaxation he cooks regularly. He says, "I like working with vegetables. I would like to think this was a matter of aesthetics or health. Probably the reason is more practical. Vegetables seem to give a wider margin of error than pastry or egg-based desserts, which I associate with disaster, or delicate meat or poultry dishes where, at present prices, there is too much at stake in being right."

AUTHOR'S NOTE: I do love a pun.

CHEESE, TOMATO, AND SOUR CREAM OMELET

From James Vorenberg

This omelet, which is believed by many to have been developed in its rudimentary form by Professor Frank E. A. Sander, one of Harvard Law School's giants of the past, may be presented in many variations. For the chopped green pepper, one may substitute mushrooms, anchovies, strips of salami or ham—one or more. In lieu of the Swiss cheese, münster, mozzarella, or provolone may be used; for the Camembert, Brie or other favorite cheese can be substituted—or you can use just one kind of cheese.

6 eggs
3 tablespoons sour cream
2 tablespoons grated Parmesan
  cheese
¼ teaspoon dill powder (optional)
½ teaspoon salt

Pinch freshly ground black pepper
1 tablespoon butter
2 large or 3 medium tomatoes, sliced
3 4×7-inch slices Swiss cheese
2 ounces Camembert cheese
1 green pepper, diced

Beat aggressively the eggs, sour cream, Parmesan, dill, salt, and pepper.

Melt butter in a 9-inch skillet. Cover bottom of skillet with sliced tomatoes and cover with Swiss. Dot with Camembert. Cook, covered, over low to medium heat until Swiss is mostly melted. Add egg mixture and sprinkle green pepper on top. Cover and cook over low to medium heat until egg mixture is firm. In covering, allow some room for mixture to rise.

Cut in wedge-shaped pieces and serve immediately with dabs of sour cream on top (optional).   SERVES 4

H. R. HALDEMAN

Author

Bob Haldeman is fit and fiftyish. Once President Nixon's chief executive officer, Bob Haldeman now lives with his wife and four children and has published a book, *The Ends of Power,* about his White House and Watergate experience.

He has "always been intrigued with cooking." He likes to cook, and now with more leisure than the White House allowed, he cooks often.

Bob Haldeman's favorite dish to cook is a perfect omelet, western in character. If his directions are followed exactly, the omelet is neither tough nor dry, but light, fluffy, and golden in color.

WESTERN OMELET

From H. R. Haldeman

3 eggs, beaten
2 tablespoons chopped cooked bacon
½ chili pepper
Handful grated Cheddar cheese
Handful grated Jack cheese
Butter
Safflower oil

Combine eggs, bacon, chili pepper, and cheeses.

Melt butter and skim off top. Use the clarified remainder with an equal part of safflower oil. There should be a spoonful of this combination. Put it in your omelet pan (no other frying pan will do) and heat it to yellow, not brown.

Put the egg mixture into the hot pan. Cook until soft, loosening side of omelet with a rubber spatula and allowing the egg to run under so all of it will be cooked. Flop the omelet over and serve.   SERVES 1 OR 2

AUTHOR'S NOTE: Mr. Haldeman mixes a pint of half clarified butter and half safflower oil and keeps it in the refrigerator for many uses, but particularly omelets.

Chapter 6

SALADS

JOHN CHANCELLOR

NBC Correspondent-Anchorman

John William Chancellor has been in America's living rooms regularly for twenty-six years. He has covered every presidential campaign and all but one important off-year election for NBC News since 1950. He has been the network's correspondent in Vienna, London, Brussels, Berlin, and Moscow (where he reported the Francis Gary Powers U-2 trial).

When he was NBC correspondent for the White House, President Johnson appointed him, in 1965, director of the Voice of America, which broadcasts around the world in thirty-eight languages.

John rarely has a sandwich at his desk; the nature of his profession calls for a good many business luncheons of rich food. But he maintains his trim waistline with regular tennis.

He sent a letter giving his original recipe for bacon, lettuce, and tomato salad and it needs no commentary from me.

BACON, LETTUCE, AND TOMATO SALAD

From John Chancellor

Cook about 1 pound bacon until it is crisp, dry it on paper towels, and break it into smallish pieces. Slab bacon is best for this, cut into very thick slices. You need lots of bacon for this salad.

Take about 4 or 5 tomatoes, skinned. Cut into eighths and squeeze out the seeds. Then chop into chunks.

Take 2 big fistfuls of escarole, which is sturdy enough not to wilt in the mixing process, and chop into smallish pieces. (I use a French machine called a Moulinette for this. A Moulinette is to a Cuisinart what a Volkswagen is to a Rolls, but it works fine for this kind of thing.)

Then in a large bowl begin mixing the bacon with the tomato chunks, blending in mayonnaise. It is best, of course, if you've made fresh mayonnaise, but store-bought will do. Bring it to the consistency of chicken or tuna salad.

Blend the escarole in last. Mix it all up, salt and pepper to taste, and put it in the refrigerator to chill. Get it cool, but not icy.

Serve it cold and provide your guests with small pieces of whole-wheat toast, buttered and quite hot. The cold salad on the hot toast is a good combination, and the BLT-on-toast flavor, one of the classic American combinations, is there in all its drugstore-counter goodness. SERVES 4, AND THEY USUALLY CRY FOR MORE.

WILLIAM PROXMIRE

Senator from Wisconsin

Twenty years ago when Senator Joseph R. McCarthy's death caused an empty Wisconsin seat in the United States Senate, Edward William Proxmire sought and won it.

Senator Proxmire's early years were spent at prep school in Pennsylvania, at Yale where he earned a degree and recognition in football and boxing, and at Harvard where he earned two master's degrees. He enlisted in the Army as a private nine months before Pearl Habor. After army duty, he worked in the investment firm of J. P. Morgan & Company in New York City, went to Wisconsin to become a resident, a newspaper reporter, a political columnist, and president of a printing company.

He is chairman of two of the Senate's most important committees—Banking, Housing and Urban Affairs, and the Joint Committee on Defense Production—and he is a member of both Appropriations and the Joint Economic committees.

The Senator jogs the nearly five miles each day from his home to his Senate office. He is careful about his looks, about his health, and about his weight.

He recommends a healthful salad—"I don't prepare it myself, but Banana Salad Tropicale, prepared in the Senators' Dining Room, is one of my favorite dishes.

"It consists of slices of banana covered with peanut butter. The dish is served with a fruit Jell-O mold, stuffed prunes, an apricot half, cottage cheese, chopped pecans and coconut, and a cream dressing."

AUTHOR'S NOTE: See Cream Dressing, page 200.

ZUCCHINI SALAD

From Clifton Daniel

Wash very clean, snip off ends, but do not peel squash. With the diagonal part of the food grater, slice thin rounds of zucchini.

2 young small zucchini squash (or 1 cup slices)
Juice of 1 small clove garlic or 1 small clove garlic, grated
½ teaspoon Dijon mustard
1 tablespoon lemon juice
3 tablespoons good olive oil

Mix garlic juice, mustard, lemon juice, and oil together with a fork or whisk and pour the sauce over the very thin slices of zucchini.　　SERVES 2

CUCUMBER SALAD

From Embassy of Germany

4 cucumbers, peeled and thinly sliced
1 tablespoon salt
Salt and pepper to taste
1 cup sour cream
Juice of ½ lemon
¼ cup chopped chives

Sprinkle cucumbers with salt and let stand for 3 hours. Drain thoroughly, season with salt and pepper to taste, and add sour cream beaten with lemon juice. Sprinkle the salad with chopped chives and chill.　　SERVES 4

HOT FRUIT SALAD

From David Eisenhower

1 12-ounce can pineapple chunks
1 12-ounce can apricots
1 12-ounce can peaches
1 12-ounce can pears
2 tablespoons butter

2 tablespoons brown sugar
½ cup canned pineapple juice
½ teaspoon (or more to taste) curry
   powder
1 teaspoon cornstarch

Drain juice from cans of pineapple, apricots, peaches, and pears and reserve.

Melt butter and add sugar, pineapple juice, reserved juices, curry powder, and cornstarch. Stir until thickened, add drained fruits, and heat over low flame. Delicious with chicken or pork.   SERVES 6

HERMAN TALMADGE

Senator from Georgia

Senator Herman Talmadge as a young lawyer twice helped his father win Geo. gia's governorship. When Eugene Talmadge, one of the South's legendary politicians, died, Herman became governor of Georgia and later United States senator.

He was married for over thirty years, to Betty Talmadge, but they are now divorced. Betty, who enjoys collecting and cooking recipes, fretted over the writing task in *How to Cook a Pig* (Simon & Shuster). When the going was particularly rough, she remembered the advice of their friend, Liz Carpenter: "Just sit down at the typewriter and do it. After all, you're not writing *War and Peace.*"

When they were married, Herman spent little time in the kitchen. But he is an experienced breakfast cook, from necessity, as he rises at 3:15 or 4:00 in the morning (he retires about 7:30 each night). He occasionally "cremates" a breakfast steak; otherwise he prepares bacon and eggs. He prefers plain cooking, particularly broiled beef and vegetables and, of course, all southern cooking. Favorites included here are Baked Country Ham, page 68, Garlic Grits, page 135, and Cucumber Mousse, which follows.

CUCUMBER MOUSSE

From the home of Senator Talmadge

5 large cucumbers
2 tablespoons gelatin
1 3-ounce package lime Jell-O
1 cup sour cream

1 cup mayonnaise
2 tablespoons lemon juice
2 cups ginger ale
Tabasco sauce to taste

Grate cucumbers and let drain for at least 1 hour (longer if time permits), reserving drained juice. Add enough water to the juice to make 2 cups of liquid. Dissolve gelatin in ¼ cup. Heat the remaining 1¾ cups and dissolve Jell-O with it. Add dissolved gelatin, sour cream, mayonnaise, lemon juice, ginger ale, and a heavy-handed dash of Tabasco sauce. After the mixture has cooked, add grated cucumbers. Pour into a large mold and refrigerate until thoroughly set. Serve with extra sour cream. SERVES 6

Chapter 7

BREADS, QUICK BREADS, AND CEREALS

ANTHONY LEWIS

Columnist, the New York Times

Tony Lewis is the author of several books, is a Pulitzer Prize winner, a columnist for the New York *Times,* and a father of three children. He was chief of the London Bureau of the *Times* from 1967 to 1972 and presently writes his column from Boston.

Once a month the Lewises have lunch, purely social, with two other couples: Dr. Howard Hiatt, dean of the Harvard School of Public Health, and his wife, and Professor James Vorenberg of Harvard Law School and Mrs. Vorenberg. It has become a men's show-off lunch, he said, with each man cooking the lunch when he is host. The last time they were together, Dr. Hiatt served his own homemade bread and mussels marinière.

Tony has a repertoire of six recipes. He was more or less forced into the kitchen when his wife, Linda, was writing a book. Tony requested more of their homemade granola and Linda said that's a good idea, why don't you make it? He found the shopping and measuring for a family-size batch of granola very time-consuming but it is easier now that he knows the recipe from memory. Just remember when you get to the health food store that there are 9 cups of raw oats and 9 other ingredients, plus safflower oil.

GRANOLA

From Anthony Lewis

9 cups raw oats
1 cup sesame seeds
1 cup sunflower seeds
1 cup chopped almonds
1 cup chopped cashew nuts
2 cups wheat germ

1 cup apricots, diced
1 cup raisins
1 cup dates, diced
1 cup honey
Safflower oil

Measure and prepare all ingredients. Where fruit is to be diced, the pieces should be quite small, as a large bite of, say, apricot, diminishes the taste of the small grains and nuts.

Pour a small amount (just enough to coat the bottom of pot) of safflower oil into a large pot. A turkey roaster is a good pan, as there are about 5 quarts of ingredients to mix. Heat oats on top of stove (the roaster pan may be used over 2 burners), stirring constantly. This heating process will take 15 or 20 minutes. Add sesame seeds, sunflower seeds, almonds, cashews, and wheat germ to oats, pour (drip) honey over all, and put pan in oven for 10 minutes (or again on top of stove), stirring frequently. Remove from heat and when mixture has cooled somewhat, stir in apricots, raisins, and dates.

Granola is now ready to eat. It will keep well in a plastic container (such as Tupperware) or quart fruit jars.　　　　　　　　　MAKES 4½ QUARTS

JALAPEÑO CORN BREAD

From Frank Ikard

3 cups corn bread mix	1 large onion, grated
3 eggs, beaten	1 No. 2 can cream-style corn
2¼ cups milk	1½ cups grated cheese
½ cup vegetable oil	5 jalapeño peppers, chopped
3 teaspoons sugar	

Combine all ingredients, pour into a 15×11-inch aluminum pan, and bake in a preheated 375° oven for 45 minutes.

ROBERT GRIFFIN

Senator from Michigan

Michigan's senior senator, Robert Griffin, has given ten years to the House of Representatives and ten years to the Senate. Senator Griffin is a solid statesman, soft-spoken, unpretentious, and conscientious about his work. He sponsors what he calls "human legislation," such as the National Student Loan program which enables millions of students to attend college. He has been married thirty years and has four children.

Both Bob and Marge Griffin enjoy the kitchen, and plain food is their preference. During their 1972 political campaign, they produced a small cookbook of their favorite recipes. It was so popular that all copies have been given away and they are reprinting it to satisfy requests from their constituents. Marge is of Scandinavian extraction and her Danish pastry (below) is a family recipe.

Bob is a serious cook—once when he was busy in the kitchen he answered the phone for an important business call. "Call me back in fifteen minutes," he said. "I'm at a crucial point in my spaghetti sauce."

"Since cooking, like politics, is the art of the possible, I tend to make my recipes as simple as possible. Our home in Michigan [Traverse City] overlooks Long Lake. It is one of the many beautiful and picturesque lakes that grace our state. Mornings there are sparkling and crisp, and I love to get up early and fix a big pancake breakfast outside for my family and our house guests."

DANISH CRESCENTS

From the home of Senator Griffin

4 cups all-purpose flour
1 teaspoon salt
1 tablespoon sugar
2 cakes yeast (crumbled in bit of cold milk)
2 eggs

1 cup milk
1 cup butter
Melted butter
Sugar, cinnamon, raisins, nuts (optional)

Combine flour, salt, 1 tablespoon sugar, yeast, eggs, milk, and butter and mix well.

Let the dough stand in refrigerator overnight. In the morning divide into 4 parts. Roll out each piece thin like pie crust. Brush with melted butter. Sprinkle with sugar and cinnamon. Add raisins and nuts.

Roll up like a jelly roll. Cut off 1-inch slices and shape them into crescents, placing them on a cookie sheet. Let rise in a warm place for 1 hour. Bake in a preheated 350° oven for 35 minutes.

When cool, frost with vanilla frosting (confectioners' sugar, butter, and vanilla), or they may be decorated with colored sugar for the holidays.

MAKES 4 DOZEN

PANCAKES WITH BEER AND BLUEBERRIES

From Senator Griffin

2 cups all-purpose flour
¼ cup sugar
3 teaspoons baking powder
Salt to taste
1 egg

¾ cup beer
½ cup milk
2 tablespoons melted butter
1 pint fresh blueberries

Mix all ingredients except blueberries in a mixer or blender. Just before you bake the pancakes on a preheated griddle, stir in blueberries.

Serve warm with blueberry syrup.   SERVES 4

NED KENWORTHY

Reporter, the New York Times

Ned Kenworthy left college teaching to be a reporter for the New York *Times* in 1950. He attacks each reporting assignment with energy and vitality and remains enthusiastic throughout. He is often assigned to dig and assemble facts for months on a major news story and excels in this kind of reporting. He is the newspaperman every reporter would like to be—hard-driving, solid, and inquisitive, with unassailable integrity.

Ned's cooking, repertoire includes fish and seafood of all kinds, as he spends much time in New England and catches flounder and sea bass—standard fare for Kenworthy vacations. Vichyssoise is also a specialty.

Ned became kitchen-savvy by helping his father, who always cooked the roast, the steaks, and regularly made bread. The Kenworthy bread needs three risings and the directions below are wonderfully clear.

BREAD

From Ned Kenworthy

2½ cups milk
8 tablespoons butter
½ cup sugar
2 teaspoons salt
2–3 cups sifted unbleached white
    flour

2 eggs, beaten
2 ¼-ounce packages dried yeast
2 cups (unsifted) whole-wheat flour

Warm milk in a saucepan. While warming, dissolve butter, sugar, and salt in the milk. When butter is melted in warm milk, pour mixture into a bowl with 2 cups of the white flour. Pour in beaten eggs and yeast (with dried yeast it is not necessary to predissolve in water). Stir this soupy mixture vigorously, or better, use an electric beater to get mixture fairly smooth.

Add whole-wheat flour. Add remaining white flour—and more if necessary, depending on God knows what—until dough becomes stiff and comes away from side of bowl. Lift onto a floured wooden board and knead for 8–10 minutes, pulling dough from edges to center and using heel of the hand for kneading.

Wash and dry bowl and lightly coat with melted butter. Place kneaded dough in bowl and turn it over to coat with butter. Place wet paper towels or a linen towel over the bowl and set it in a warm (about 80°) place. It should rise until size of dough has doubled, about 1–1½ hours. When dough has risen, push doubled fist from top to bottom of bowl. This will deflate the dough.

Knead lightly in bowl for 1 minute and cover with damp cloth as before. Let rise until almost double, usually 45 minutes to 1 hour. Do not punch again.

Lift dough to lightly floured board, cut into 3 equal sections, shape it to fit pans, cover with cloth, and let rest for 10–15 minutes. Place dough in pans, shaping it. Brush tops lightly with melted butter.

Place pans in a preheated 400° oven. Leave it for 15 minutes at this temperature. Turn oven down to 375° and bake 25–30 minutes longer.

Turn bread out on rack. Thump bottom of loaves with finger. If the sound is hollow, bread is done. If not, return to oven for another 5–10 minutes.

Allow to cool somewhat, cut 2 or 3 slices, butter, and make a pig of yourself.

MAKES 3 LOAVES

AUTHOR'S NOTE ABOUT BAKING BREAD: Baking bread is a simple job but you must stay home half a day to do it. The actual time involved in preparing the dough is minimal, but the rising time requires hours.

Everyone has his own method for all the fussy small details required in the preparation of bread. One of mine is to put the bowl of faintly warm mixed dough into the oven which is also faintly warm. In this secure place, drafts and children cannot disturb it. Then, from time to time, I light the oven for just a minute or two to keep the temperature barely warm.

If you don't want to do this, you can follow Arab practice: Wrap the kneaded bowl of dough like a baby, lightly but completely, in a lightweight wool blanket or shawl, and set it in the sun.

The first time you make bread, the task seems endless, but when you have perfected all the details, the preparation becomes mindless and routine. You will find that you can make the bread in between several other household tasks.

SPOON BREAD

From Representative Montgomery

2 eggs, separated	2 tablespoons butter
1½ cups water	1 cup sweet milk
1 teaspoon salt	Salt and pepper to taste
1 cup white corn meal	

Beat egg whites until stiff and set aside. Beat egg yolks in separate bowl.

Bring water and salt to boiling point. Gradually stir in corn meal. Cook and stir until thickened and smooth. Remove from heat and add butter, milk, and well-beaten egg yolks, mixing well. Add salt and pepper. Fold in egg whites. Pour into greased baking dish about 1½ quart size and bake in a preheated 350° oven for 30 minutes or until firm.   SERVES 4

AUTHOR'S NOTE: This is a delicious and dependable recipe for spoon bread.

RICHARD CLARK

Senator from Iowa

Dick Clark learned how to maneuver in Congress when he was administrative assistant to then Congressman, now Senator, John Culver of Iowa. In this capacity from 1965 to 1972, he made valuable acquaintances and polished political connections in Iowa. In November 1972 he ran for the Senate and won, crediting his success to a walk from one end of Iowa to the other.

"During a political campaign, it's often difficult to get good home cooking, as many candidates will undoubtedly agree. I was more fortunate, however, since my campaign consisted of a thirteen-hundred-mile walk across Iowa, and I often stayed with Iowans in their homes. The result was a lot of good home-style food—all of which prevented any significant weight loss during the walk. Among my fond memories of that campaign in 1972 are these cinnamon rolls which were baked by members of my campaign staff and brought to me at various points on the road. I remember one particular incident when my staff, laden with rolls and coffee, met me at six A.M., just as I was walking into Cedar Rapids. Believe me, having those rolls in the morning helped make the miles seem shorter during the day.

"I only hope this recipe brings as much pleasure to others as it has to me."

CINNAMON ROLLS

From Senator Clark

¾ cup milk
½ cup granulated sugar
3 tablespoons shortening
1 teaspoon salt
1 cake compressed yeast
¼ cup warm water

1 egg
4 cups all-purpose flour
⅓ cup melted butter
1¾ cups brown sugar
1 teaspoon cinnamon
3 tablespoons butter

Scald milk and pour over granulated sugar, shortening, and salt in a mixing bowl. Cool to lukewarm.

Soften yeast in warm water and add to milk mixture; add egg. Add 2 cups flour and beat vigorously. Add rest of flour, kneading well. Form into a ball, grease the top, cover, and let rise until doubled in bulk.

Roll out on floured board to about ½ inch thick. Mix together melted butter, 1 cup brown sugar, and cinnamon and spread over dough. Roll up.

Butter a pan with 3 tablespoons butter and sprinkle with the remaining ¾ cup brown sugar.

Cut dough in 1-inch slices and place cut side down on mix in pan. Let rise until doubled.

Bake in a preheated 400° oven for 30–35 minutes.   MAKES 3 DOZEN

HOWARD HIATT

Dean of the Harvard School of Public Health

Howard H. Hiatt is a slim elegant man who would look at home in one of those exclusive British gentleman's clubs. He earned his M.D. from Harvard in 1948 and in addition to research and practice in medicine, went on to teach and become dean of the Harvard School of Public Health. His department is responsible for one of the finest nutrition departments in the world.

Dean Hiatt puts much of himself into his work. He spent a year in England studying the British system of medicine, and he tries to translate this experience into practical help for the poor and aged who cannot afford the ever-upward cost of medical care in the United States.

Dr. Hiatt is one of the members of the Boston area Saturday luncheon group where the men cook the luncheon and the women merely enjoy it. One of his specialties is home-baked bread.

"From time to time, I turn to bread baking, for kneading proves a particularly effective way to work off administrative frustrations."

SHREDDED WHEAT BREAD

From Howard Hiatt

1½ packages active dry yeast
¼ cup lukewarm water
1 teaspoon sugar
2 cups boiling water
4 shredded wheat biscuits
3 tablespoons butter

1 tablespoon salt
2 tablespoons sugar
⅓ cup honey
4½ cups (approximately) all-
    purpose flour
1 cup whole-wheat flour

Proof yeast in ¼ cup lukewarm water and 1 teaspoon sugar.

Pour boiling water over shredded wheat, butter, salt, 2 tablespoons sugar, and honey. Mix and when lukewarm, add the yeast mixture, which should be spongy. Add flour, 1 cup at a time, until the dough is stiff enough to work. Knead gently in the bowl for a few minutes, cover with a warm damp towel, and let rise until doubled in bulk, 2–3 hours.

Push down the dough, let rest for 5 minutes, and knead another 3–4 minutes. Form into 2 loaves and place in greased loaf pans. Butter the top of the loaves and allow to rise until doubled in bulk.

Bake in a preheated 400° oven for 15 minutes. Reduce oven temperature to 350° and bake for ½ hour longer. Remove from pans and replace in oven for 3 or 4 minutes to brown the sides and bottom.   MAKES 2 SMALL LOAVES

SOUR MILK PANCAKES

From Robert McClory

2 cups all-purpose flour
2 teaspoons baking powder
4 tablespoons sugar
1 teaspoon salt
2 eggs, well beaten

1 tablespoon cooking oil
2 cups sour milk or thinned
    buttermilk (thin buttermilk with
    water in which ½ teaspoon soda
    is dissolved)

Sift together flour, baking powder, sugar, and salt. Add eggs, oil, and sour milk and mix well. Cook as you would any pancake on a griddle or Teflon frying pan.

Mr. McClory says this will serve 10 adults on a diet or a family of 4.

AUTHOR'S NOTE: To make sour milk add 2 teaspoons vinegar to whole milk and allow it to sit in a warm place. It is best if you make the sour milk several days in advance so that it gradually cultures and thickens.

WILLIAM V. SHANNON

U. S. Ambassador

As John Kennedy was to American politics, William Vincent Shannon is to the world of the intelligentsia and the literary. An Irish Catholic from Massachusetts, he attended public schools and eventually earned an advanced degree from Harvard, then continued his career writing for prestigious publications including *The Economist* of London, *Harper's, Atlantic, New Statesman,* and *American Heritage.* For thirteen years he was a member of the Editorial Board of the New York *Times,* earning the label in a *New York* magazine piece "the conscience of The New York Times." He is now United States ambassador to Ireland.

Before the Shannons became America's representative in Ireland, they entertained informally in Washington—usually six or eight friends, with emphasis on good food, wine, and relaxation. Bill remembers one evening a few days after the resignation of Richard Nixon when his party was not relaxed. The guests included both liberal Democrats, conservative Republicans, and a foreign ambassador. This ambassador, fascinated with a democracy that could force a President's resignation, introduced the subject. One of the Republican guests rose quickly, offered a toast to the foreign policy accomplishments of the Nixon Administration, and as he sat down, the chair broke and he crashed to the floor. Liz Shannon, a Democrat, recovered quickly with, "That will teach you, George not to toast President Nixon in this house."

Bill admits to no hobbies except reading and cooking, with emphasis on baking. He has a collection of bread cookbooks and specializes in such delicacies as Irish soda bread, potato bread (from an Irish cookbook), popovers, wheat breads, and brioche.

Brioche is known as the king of the breads and is extremely difficult to make. The secret is the handling of the dough (the Shannon children love slapping it about) and the baker's technique is all-important. Bill's mastery of this is unsurpassed.

FRENCH BRIOCHE

From William Shannon*

1 package yeast	*1 cup soft butter*
Lukewarm water	*1 teaspoon salt*
2–3 tablespoons sugar	*7 eggs*
4 cups (approximately) sifted flour	*½ cup milk, scalded and cooled*

Soften yeast in ⅓ cup lukewarm water. Add 1 teaspoon sugar and 1 cup flour. Mix and then knead until smooth. Place ball of dough in a bowl and cover with lukewarm water. Let rise until ball floats in water, about 1 hour or less.

Put remaining flour in a large bowl. Add the ball of dough, ½ the butter, remaining sugar, salt, and 2 of the eggs, slightly beaten. Mix well with the fingers, adding enough milk to give a soft, nonsticky dough. Turn out on a lightly floured board and knead until smooth.

Work in the remaining butter and 2 more eggs. Repeat the kneading. Lift the dough and slap or bang it on the table until it is very smooth.

Add 2 more eggs, work them into the dough, and repeat the kneading and banging on the table.

Shape the dough into a ball and place it in a greased bowl. Cover and let rise in a warm place (80°–85°) until double in bulk.

Punch and stir the dough down. Shape into a ball, place in a clean greased bowl, cover tightly with foil, and chill overnight or slightly longer.

To shape the brioche, turn the dough out onto a floured board. Cut off about ⅙ and reserve for topknots of buns. Divide remainder of the dough into 18–24 portions and shape each into a ball. Place in greased brioche pans or muffin tins (2¾ × 1¼ inches deep). Cut reserved dough into the same number of small balls. Dampen a finger slightly and make a depression in the center of each large ball. Place a small ball in each of the depressions. Cover and let rise in a warm place until double in bulk, or about 1 hour.

Lightly beat remaining egg and brush over the tops of the brioche. Place on rack near bottom of a preheated 450° oven and bake until well browned, about 15 minutes.   MAKES 18–24

* From *The New York Times Cook Book,* by Craig Claiborne.

ROBERT T. STAFFORD

Senator from Vermont

Robert T. Stafford entered Vermont politics when he was twenty-five years old. He later became lieutenant governor, then governor, and was his state's only congressman for ten years when in 1971 he was appointed senator to fill an unexpired term.

The 6'2" tall senator describes himself as an outdoorsman who enjoys skiing, hiking, and camping. And for bridging the distance between Vermont and the nation's capital, he pilots a small plane.

Senator Stafford honors pancakes, calls them Green Mountain Pancakes, and serves them with Vermont maple syrup. His staff explains "Green Mountain"— Vermont's mountains are green all year around because of the evergreen trees which cover them.

GREEN MOUNTAIN PANCAKES

From Senator Stafford

1½ cups sifted all-purpose flour	1 egg
2½ teaspoons baking powder	¾–1 cup milk
1 tablespoon sugar	3 tablespoons melted butter or
¾ teaspoon salt	margarine

Sift together flour, baking powder, sugar, and salt. Add beaten egg and milk. Fold in melted butter and cook on medium-hot grill; turn when pancakes begin to bubble. Serve with butter and Vermont maple syrup.

RAYMOND PROBST

Swiss Ambassador

Swiss Ambassador Raymond Probst is a hard-driving, energetic, shrewd man. Humor and intelligence are the main ingredients of his personality. He was born in Geneva in 1919, educated in Baltic and Swiss schools, and earned a law degree from Berne University. He is an expert in international negotiations and trade and his diplomatic career made travel possible in more than twenty countries.

The Probsts notice many changes since their first assignment to Washington twenty years ago. "Washington is a cultural heaven, compared to our stay here in the fifties. And we notice with interest that your food habits have become more sophisticated. Americans have discovered wine—your wine is very good—and"—with a smile—"we no longer see people in restaurants drinking a big glass of milk with their steak."

During this discussion we were having a luncheon in the small embassy dining room. The excellent menu included:

Cheese Soufflé

Geschnetzeltes and Roesti
(veal ragout with a "cake" of pan-fried potatoes)

Green Salad

Pears Hélène (stewed in syrup and covered with a rich chocolate sauce)

Pear Brandy (a clear delicious liquid with a beautiful pear fragrance)

Ambassador Probst commented: "We are asked to eat too much in this diplomatic life, and if we note that a party has been catered, we eat very sparingly. But conversely, if a hostess has taken great care to serve homemade specialties, we eat everything with enjoyment. It is a welcome rarity for us to have a night off, and then we eat sparingly at home—soup or a supper of cold meats, bread, and fruit. We often take Birchermuesli when we are slimming." The recipe follows.

"LITTLE MIXTURE" (Birchermuesli)

From Embassy of Switzerland

3 tablespoons sweetened condensed
  milk
3 tablespoons oat flakes (the quick-
  cooking kind)
Juice of 1 or 2 lemons and 1 orange

6 apples, 1 orange, 1 banana, all
  sliced, or 1 pound mixed berries
  (strawberries, blueberries, etc.)
½ cup chopped nuts
½ cup cream (optional)

Mix condensed milk with the oat flakes and the lemon and orange juice. Add fruit and nuts and a little cream if you wish.   SERVES 4

AUTHOR'S NOTE: *Muesli* translates literally "mess" or "mixture," and *Bircher* is a well-known Zurich doctor who runs a fashionable, very expensive "fat" clinic where Europe's wealthy do their "slimming" together. Birchermuesli is not particularly low-calorie but is a healthy food. Additionally, hunger is quickly satisfied and there is no need to eat again for hours.

SPECIAL GRAHAM CRACKERS

From the home of J. Carter Brown

¼ cup very soft dark brown sugar
1 teaspoon cinnamon
¼ cup melted butter (melt it just to
  point of softening and melting)

12 or 18 graham crackers

Mix brown sugar and cinnamon together. Mix this sugar mixture with melted butter and spread on graham crackers. Put the crackers under the broiler (use toaster oven if you wish) for 1 or 2 minutes until the butter-sugar begins to bubble. Remove from oven and serve warm.

This is a simple but quite delicious treat for tea.   SERVES 4

ART HOPPE

Columnist, San Francisco Chronicle

Time magazine says, "Art Hoppe at his best is unbeatable." He is called the best political satirist in the country. Art has been with the San Francisco *Chronicle* since 1949 when he started as a copy boy. He is now a syndicated political columnist-humorist. He authored several books; his latest, *Miss Lollipop and the Doom Machine*. His hobbies are sailing, skiing, tennis, outdoor drinking, and sandwich making.

In a letter, he writes: "Probably my favorite recipe is one that's been handed down in my family for generations. When I was just a tad, my Aunt Addie (who is admittedly none too reliable) told me that this particular recipe was first brought over to this country by my great-great-great-grandfather, Jeremiah Cobey, who emigrated from the Isle of Man in 1763 after he lost his entire herd of Manx sheep in an outbreak of coreopsis. In any event here, for what it's worth, is the recipe."

MANX GHLUM

From Art Hoppe

2 slices white Wonder bread
2 tablespoons Mary Ellen grape jelly

2 tablespoons Skippy peanut butter
(crunchy, if desired)

Take 1 slice of bread and lay it flat on counter top or similar structure. Place jelly on bread. Spread carefully, making sure not to go over the edges. Place peanut butter on other slice of bread. Spread carefully, making sure that the entire surface is covered and no "white spots" remain. Now, with quick motion, flip the slice with the peanut butter *on top of* the slice bearing the jelly. *Under no circumstance* attempt to flip the slice bearing the jelly on top of the slice that is peanut-buttered.　　　　SERVES 1

AUTHOR'S NOTE:　　The etymology of the word *ghlum* is unclear.

Chapter 8

CONDIMENTS AND SAUCES

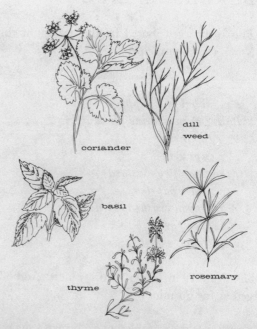

coriander

dill weed

basil

rosemary

thyme

IN PRAISE OF HERBS

There is interesting literature from Pliny to Craig Claiborne on the importance and use of herbs. Herbs are important in medicine, food, flavoring, fragrance, aphrodisiacs, and magic.

Until the Crusades, men dominated the herbs, and only when they went off to their wars were women allowed to tend the special gardens. The gardens were always carefully and beautifully managed.

Charlemagne had one of the most famous herb gardens. The learned monk Alcuin came from Ireland to teach Charlemagne all that he knew of herbs. "What is an herb?" asked the monk of Charlemagne, and the Emperor answered, "The friend of the physician and the praise of cooks."

Before you plant your own garden it might be worthwhile to visit the herb garden at the Cloisters on the Hudson in New York (home of the famed Unicorn tapestries), or the sweet small garden of herbs at Blair House in Williamsburg, Virginia, or the practical one at the National Cathedral in Washington, D.C. And in the near future the Herb Society of America will plant an herb garden at the National Arboretum.

There are no words to describe the taste of fresh dill in a salad or a sauce for spring lamb, or the sprays of tarragon or marjoram in chicken, or basil from your garden in the pesto sauce. Truly, these fragrant green plants are the secret of the world's finest cuisine.

BARBECUE SAUCE

This is not contributed by the donors of this book, but is an old and authentic North Carolina recipe.

1 small onion, chopped
Butter or margarine for sautéing
½ cup vinegar
1½ cups water
1 teaspoon dry mustard
1 teaspoon paprika
½ teaspoon crushed dried red
  pepper (or to taste)
2 teaspoons salt

Tabasco sauce or liquid hot pepper
  sauce to taste
Chili powder to taste
1 tablespoon Worchestershire sauce
1 tablespoon black pepper
2 cloves garlic, minced
Juice of 1 lemon
½ cup tomato ketchup (optional,
  but makes sauce thicker)

Sauté onion in butter until golden. Add all other ingredients and simmer together for 20 minutes.   MAKES 3 CUPS

NOTE: Add 1 tablespoon brown sugar if you are barbecuing chicken.

GREEN SAUCE (Sauce Verte)

From White House Chef Henry Haller*

1 bunch watercress, washed and
  dried
½ tablespoon Worcestershire sauce
6 drops hot pepper sauce
1 teaspoon salt
⅛ teaspoon white pepper
1 teaspoon monosodium glutamate
  (optional)

1 teaspoon Dijon mustard
2 cups sour cream
1½ cups mayonnaise
2 drops green food coloring
  (optional)

Cut off bottom third of watercress stems and discard. Chop remaining cress and place in a glass or stainless steel bowl with Worcestershire, hot pepper sauce, and salt. Mix together and let stand at room temperature for ½ hour.

* From William Rice, the Washington *Post*.

Place a square of cheesecloth in another bowl (2 quart size) and spoon cress plus juice onto cheesecloth. Gather corners together, turn cloth, and gently squeeze out juice. There should be no more than ½ cup. Discard any excess as well as cheesecloth and watercress (or use watercress in a mixed green salad). Add white pepper, monosodium glutamate, and mustard and blend into liquid. Add sour cream and stir with a whisk to combine with juice. When of an even consistency, stir in mayonnaise. Taste and adjust flavor. Add food coloring and stir in. Serve at room temperature. Excellent with fish.

HOLLANDAISE SAUCE

From the home of Tom Wicker

¼ pound butter
4 egg yolks
2 teaspoons lemon juice (or
    vinegar)

Pinch salt
Pinch white pepper

Divide butter into 3 parts. Into the top of a double boiler, place egg yolks and 1 part of the butter. Over hot but not boiling water, stir rapidly and constantly with a wooden spoon until the butter is melted. Then add the second piece of butter and, as the mixture thickens and the butter melts, add the third piece, stirring constantly. Do not allow the water over which the sauce is cooking to come to a boil.

When the butter is melted and the sauce is well mixed, remove the pan from the heat and continue beating for at least 2 more minutes. Add lemon juice (or vinegar) and salt and pepper. Replace the pan over the hot (but still not boiling) water for 1 or 2 minutes, beating all the while. Remove from heat at once. Should the mixture curdle, immediately beat in 1 or 2 tablespoons boiling water, beating constantly, in order to rebind the emulsion.   MAKES 1 CUP

AUTHOR'S NOTE: If you haven't awakened at eight o'clock to prepare this sauce for brunch as Pam Wicker suggests, you might make a somewhat quicker blender version of hollandaise, in which case you could sleep until eight-fifteen.

BLENDER HOLLANDAISE

From Senator Brock

½ pound butter	¼ teaspoon salt
2 tablespoons lemon juice	Pinch cayenne
4 egg yolks	

Heat butter to bubbling. Just before it is ready, warm lemon juice and place in blender with yolks, salt, and cayenne. Blend briefly, and immediately add hot butter in slow, steady stream while blending at slow speed.   MAKES 1½ CUPS

AUTHOR'S NOTE about the old-fashioned method of making hollandaise (Tom Wicker recipe) and the blender way (Senator Brock recipe):

The *Wicker* sauce method is subject to human error, but if directions are carefully followed, the sauce, both texture and taste, is beautiful.

The *Brock* sauce is more failure-proof, but sometimes the consistency is somewhat rubbery.

SWEET TOMATO PICKLE

From Frank Ikard

8 quarts (10 pounds) sliced green tomatoes (⅛-inch slices)	1 cup salt
	1 quart vinegar
2 quarts sliced onions (⅛-inch slices)	4 cups sugar
	6 tablespoons mixed pickling spice

Place tomatoes and onions in a large bowl and sprinkle with salt. Cover with a large plate, then place a heavy weight over it to hold it down. Let stand overnight, then wash and drain tomato mixture 3 times in cold water. Place in a kettle and add vinegar and sugar. Tie spice in a cheesecloth bag and add. Simmer, uncovered, until tomatoes and onions are tender, about 5 minutes. Remove spice bag. Pour at once into clean hot preserve jars and adjust covers as manufacturer directs. Set jars on a wire rack in a covered deep kettle with boiling water to cover tops of jars 1 inch. Process takes 30 minutes, counting time from when active boiling resumes.   MAKES 6–7 PINTS

MAURITIAN CHUTNEY (Cotomili)

From the home of Robert Keeley

3 unpeeled fresh tomatoes, chopped
well
1 fresh green chili, chopped

½ cup chopped fresh coriander
2 tablespoons chopped scallion,
chive, or onion

Mix all ingredients together. Let them stand for a while and serve with Mauritian Lentils (Dholl), and Mauritian Fish (Vinday), page 28.

This is also a good accompaniment to curry, cold meat, shepherd's pie, etc. Americans quickly become addicted to Cotomili and eat it with a variety of foods.   MAKES 1½ CUPS

HOUSE DRESSING FOR GREEN SALAD

From William Safire

Bill Safire always makes the house dressing, a vinaigrette with the substitution, if he has an open bottle, of wine for some of the vinegar (use ½ vinegar, including some wine, and ½ oil).

1 cup vinegar
1 cup olive oil (or safflower oil if
you are worried about cholesterol)
1 teaspoon dry English mustard
(sprinkle this or it will form balls)
5 whole cloves garlic, peeled and
left in jar of dressing

½ teaspoon horseradish
½ teaspoon oregano
½ teaspoon basil
½ teaspoon dill
½ teaspoon freeze-dried chives
Salt and freshly ground black pepper
to taste

CREAM DRESSING

⅓ cup cream chese
2 teaspoons grated orange rind
Juice of ½ orange
3 tablespoons sugar

Pinch nutmeg
Pinch cinnamon
1 cup mayonnaise
⅓ cup heavy cream

Use a fork to mash and soften the cream cheese. Add orange rind and juice, sugar, nutmeg and cinnamon. Lastly, add mayonnaise and cream.

MAKES 2 CUPS

AUTHOR'S NOTE: This is my recipe for a very usable dressing for fruit or gelatin salads.

GREEN SAUCE FOR VEGETABLES

From Howard Hiatt

2 teaspoons Dijon-style mustard
1 cup fresh parsley
6–8 scallions, using much of the tops
¼ cup wine vinegar

½ cup salad oil
2 eggs, lightly beaten
Salt to taste

Blend all of the above together and serve with vegetables: good with boiled potatoes, some salads, cauliflower, zucchini.

MAKES 1 CUP

Chapter 9

DESSERTS

PETER RAMSBOTHAM

Former British Ambassador

Sir Peter and Lady Ramsbotham were three-year occupants of the British Embassy in Washington. Sir Peter has recently been appointed Governor General of Bermuda, and young Ambassador Peter Jay takes his place in the Capital.

The Ramsbothams entertained often in the Massachusetts Avenue mansion next door to the official residence of the Vice-president of the United States. Twenty-five guests can sit comfortably in the embassy dining room and the ballroom accommodates eighty for dinner. Dinners honoring Queen Elizabeth's state visits are held in the ballroom, with guests overflowing into the lovely gardens.

The Ramsbothams' parties usually had a theme, often historic. One recent party was to honor the son-in-law of Sir Winston Churchill, Honorable Christopher Soames, on the anniversary of the elder statesman's death. Pipers from Sir Winston's regiment, the Fourth Hussars, with their silver trumpets, were flown from England for the occasion.

Lady Ramsbotham agrees that everyone borrows from the French when elegant food is needed for an important party. She would not want to serve typically English food, as it is somewhat heavy, she said. Here is one of her personal favorite recipes, enjoyed over the years.

APRICOT CREAM SUPREME

From Embassy of Great Britain

4 teaspoons (1 envelope) gelatin
½ cup cold canned apricot juice
1 ½ cups hot canned apricot juice
Pinch salt
½ cup sugar
2 tablespoons lemon juice

½ teaspoon almond essence
½ cup light cream
½ cup heavy cream
1 cup shredded, toasted coconut
2 cups sliced or puréed apricots

Combine unflavored gelatin and cold juice. Mix thoroughly. Add hot juice and stir until gelatin is dissolved. Add salt, sugar, lemon juice, and almond essence. Mix well, add light cream, and chill until mixture thickens.

Beat heavy cream until mixture is thick and shiny but not stiff. Fold this and ¾ cup toasted coconut into chilled mixture (see note 1). Spoon into molds. Chill until firm. When ready to serve, unmold and garnish with apricots and remaining coconut. SERVES 6

AUTHOR'S NOTES:

1. The dish is also excellent without coconut. At this point, I fold in about 1 cup puréed stewed apricots (see note 2), which makes the dessert rich and apricoty.

2. One can use canned fruit, but the dessert is quite delicious when dried apricots have been stewed for 30 minutes with 2 cups water and ½ cup sugar for each 2 cups apricots; then the apricots are puréed in a blender.

3. Lady Ramsbotham is a great lady, indeed. And of all the recipes in this book, I find that I keep repeating her apricot cream. For me, it is delicious and rich and creamy, yet light, which a dessert should be after a complete dinner.

ORANGE À L'ARABE

From the home of Russell Baker

16 seedless oranges	*1 vanilla bean*
1 ¼ cups sugar	*2 or 3 ounces Grand Marnier*

Using a potato peeler, peel the skins from 8 of the oranges. Slice these peels as finely as you can. They should be no larger than toothpicks. Cover with water and bring to a boil in a saucepan. Drain and re-cover with cold water. Boil and drain. Cover a third time with cold water. Add sugar and vanilla bean and simmer the slivers until they become translucent and the liquid is syrupy. Set aside.

Only peel from 8 of the oranges is used for the sauce. The rest of the orange peel should be discarded. Use a thin, very sharp knife and peel all (orange skin, white skin and membrane) from all the oranges. Cut the oranges crossways (round wheels) into slices ¼ inch thick. Pour the orange peel syrup and Grand Marnier over the orange slices and refrigerate (cover first) a few hours before serving.

This is light and delicious and can be made a day or more in advance.

SERVES 12

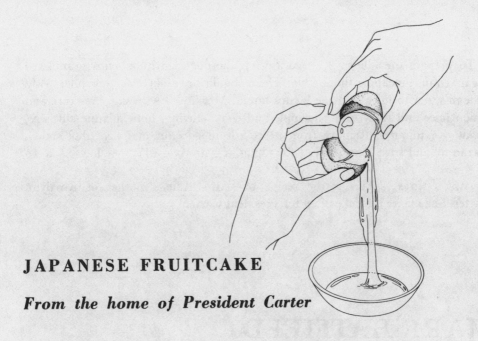

JAPANESE FRUITCAKE

From the home of President Carter

CAKE:
1 cup butter
2 cups granulated sugar
4 eggs, separated
3 cups flour
1 tablespoon baking powder
1 cup milk
1 teaspoon vanilla extract
1 teaspoon nutmeg
1 teaspoon cinnamon
½ teaspoon cloves
¾ cup raisins

FILLING:
4 tablespoons cornstarch
2 cups granulated sugar
1 20-ounce can crushed pineapple
Grated rind and juice of 2 lemons
2 cups grated unsweetened coconut

GLAZE:
3 cups confectioners' sugar
2 tablespoons lemon juice
2 tablespoons (approximately) water

Cream butter and 2 cups granulated sugar until light. Add egg yolks and beat well.

Sift flour and baking powder together and add this to batter alternately with milk. Beat in vanilla. Beat egg whites until stiff and fold into batter.

Line bottom of 2 9-inch cake pans with waxed paper and spoon about ⅔ of batter into 1 pan. Fold nutmeg, cinnamon, cloves, and raisins into remaining batter and spoon into second pan. Bake in a preheated 375° oven for 35–40 minutes, until cakes are done. Cool on wire racks in pans for 10 minutes. Turn cakes out onto racks and cool completely.

Split each layer in half. Place raisin-filled layer, cut side up, on bottom. Cover with ¼ of filling. Top with plain layer; top with another ¼ of filling. Repeat, ending with filling.

(Or filling can be used between layers and top of cake can be glazed. Combine confectioners' sugar, lemon juice, and water and spread over cake.)

To prepare the filling: Mix cornstarch thoroughly with 2 cups granulated sugar. Drain pineapple thoroughly. There should be about 1⅓ cups juice. Add enough water to juice to make 2 cups liquid. Mix liquid with sugar mixture and lemon juice and rind. Add pineapple and cook, stirring, until mixture thickens, about 5–7 minutes. Remove from heat. Stir in coconut and cool thoroughly. Use to fill and frost cake (or just for filling, if glaze is used).   SERVES 8–10

AUTHOR'S NOTE: This is the recipe of "Miss Allie," mother of Rosalynn Carter. She makes the cake often for President Carter.

MARK HATFIELD

Senator from Oregon

Senator Mark Hatfield came from hard-working parents and his own ambition was built on this ethic. His father was a railroader, and his mother a schoolteacher.

Mark became a teacher and dean of students at Willamette University in Oregon, got his M.A. at Stanford, joined the Navy, and entered politics to become at thirty-six the youngest governor in the history of Oregon.

He is a liberal Republican and was a supporter of Eisenhower. He is six feet tall, an excellent speaker, and a cook from time to time. He wrote:

"Before providing you with a favorite recipe, I should tell you I am married to the author of several cookbooks, the operator of cooking schools in Washington, D.C. and in Oregon, and a terrific cook. I must be very careful, therefore, about laying claim to any recipes rightfully those of Antoinette.

"Probably my favorite recipe is one for ice cream. I admit to having an unsatiable sweet tooth. This recipe came about from a tradition of the Hatfields in spending our Sunday evenings with friends, the Carl Collins, in Salem, Oregon. Each week, Carl and I would take turns making various new kinds of ice cream recipes, and then the four of us would consume what we had made. While Carl and I did not rival Baskin-Robbins in the total number of flavors we dreamed up, I think we probably ate enough in volume to equal a week's sales at any ice cream store. The tradition continues now on New Year's Eve, when the Collins join us at our home on the coast to test each other's mettle with a new ice cream recipe.

"Although we have tried many different combinations, one of the earlier ones still stands as best. It is simple enough that it can be made by any person who loves ice cream, but has been leery of complicated recipes."

MARK'S SUNDAY NIGHT ICE CREAM

From Senator Hatfield

1 quart milk
1 quart light cream
3 teaspoons vanilla extract

1 ½ cups sugar
Pinch salt

Mix and freeze according to freezer directions. This will fit in a 1-gallon cylinder of electric ice cream freezer.   SERVES 8

CARROT BREAD

From Anthony Lewis

4 eggs, beaten
2 cups sugar
1 ¼ cups salad oil
3 cups unsifted all-purpose flour
2 teaspoons baking powder

1 ½ teaspoons baking soda
¼ teaspoon salt
2 teaspoons cinnamon
2 cups finely shredded carrot

Add sugar gradually to beaten eggs, beating until thick. Add oil gradually and continue beating until thoroughly combined. Stir in flour, baking powder, soda, salt, and cinnamon until mixture is smooth. Stir in carrots until well blended. Turn into 2 well-greased 5×9-inch loaf pans, filling no more than ⅔ full. Bake in a preheated 350° oven for 1 hour for large loaves, 45 minutes for small, or until cake tester comes out clean.   MAKES 2 LOAVES

Further note from cook Lewis: The only hard part is grating the carrots, which is done by hand and just takes time. (Incidentally, and happily, the carrots just seem to make the result moist and good—it doesn't taste like carrots.) When I made this, I used a hand mixer rather than electric. That worked well, but I don't know whether that really mattered or not.

CREAM CHEESE FROSTING

From Anthony Lewis

1 8-ounce package cream cheese   *1 teaspoon vanilla extract*
1 tablespoon butter or margarine   *1 pound confectioners' sugar*

Blend cream cheese, butter, and vanilla until light and creamy. Add sugar until the mixture is of spreading consistency. Good on Carrot Bread to make it Carrot Cake.

JAMES A. McCLURE

Senator from Idaho

Senator McClure might be called a typical politician, having come up through the state legislature, practiced law, and joined the "right" organizations— Masons, Elks, American Legion, etc.

He has a wife and three children and was elected to Congress in 1966. He became a Republican senator in 1972 and was considered an asset to President Nixon's campaign.

McClure's Senate campaign was something of a "potato race," as the famous Idaho vegetable helped bring about his victory. McClure accused his Democratic opponent of being "antipotato," since any man who would boycott lettuce would do the same for the potato.

Senator McClure gets so many requests for "favorite recipes" that he has printed a formal, autographed card for his ginger snaps.

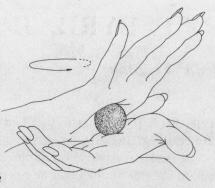

GINGER SNAPS

From Senator McClure

1 egg	1 teaspoon cinnamon
¾ cup brown sugar	1 teaspoon ginger
¾ cup molasses	¼ teaspoon salt
¾ cup shortening	¼ teaspoon cloves
3 cups all-purpose flour	Granulated sugar for coating
½ teaspoon baking soda	

Blend egg, brown sugar, molasses, and shortening. Sift together flour, soda, cinnamon, ginger, salt, and cloves. Mix dry ingredients with sugar mixture. Roll into balls and coat with sugar. Bake in a preheated 375° oven for 10–12 minutes or until done. MAKES 3½ DOZEN

CAKELESS FRUITCAKE

From Frank Ikard

½ pound whole candied cherries	2 cups pecan halves
1 pound dates, halved	¼ teaspoon salt
6 slices candied pineapple, cut in chunks	½ teaspoon vanilla extract
1 4-ounce box dry coconut	1 13-ounce can sweetened condensed milk

Mix all ingredients thoroughly in a large bowl. Grease 1 large bread pan and 2 small ones. Line pan with waxed paper. Grease the paper thoroughly. Press mixture firmly into pan. Bake in a preheated 325° oven for 10 minutes. Reduce temperature to 300° and bake another 30 minutes or until top begins to brown. Cool cakes on wire rack. Remove as soon as they begin to cool, or waxed paper will cling. MAKES 1½ LOAVES

HARRY F. BYRD, JR.

Senator from Virginia

Senator Harry F. Byrd, Jr., belongs to the Byrd family that has ruled Virginia politics for fifty years. Senator Byrd is sixty-four and has thick silvery hair. He claims history, particularly Abraham Lincoln history, as his hobby. Senator Byrd is so proud of his state's apples that he has put together a booklet of his favorite apple recipes. Apple crisp, pie, and applesauce cake are from this collection.

Care should be taken to select somewhat tart, hard, juicy apples, such as the Rome, York, or Stayman apple, all of which are grown on the senator's farm in Winchester, Virginia, an hour from Washington.

OLD-FASHIONED APPLE PIE

From Senator Byrd

PASTRY:
- 2½ cups all-purpose flour
- 1 teaspoon salt
- ¾ cup shortening (lard or vegetable shortening)
- 5 tablespoons (approximately) cold water

FILLING:
- 8 large tart Byrd apples, thinly sliced (York, Stayman, Rome)
- 1 cup sugar
- 1 teaspoon cinnamon
- ½ teaspoon nutmeg
- ⅛ teaspoon salt
- 1 teaspoon lemon juice
- 1 teaspoon butter

To prepare the pastry: Sift flour and salt together. Add ½ of the shortening and cut with 2 knives or pastry blender until mixture looks like corn meal. Add remaining shortening and continue cutting until particles are size of large pea. Sprinkle water, 1 tablespoon at a time, over mixture. With a fork, work lightly together until all particles are moistened and in small lumps. Add just enough water to moisten. Press dampened particles together into a ball. Do not handle dough any more than necessary. When ready to bake, divide dough in half, roll out each half and line a 9-inch pie plate.

To prepare the filling: Fill pie shell with sliced apples. Mix sugar, cinnamon, nutmeg, salt, and lemon juice together and sprinkle over apples. Dot with butter. Moisten edge of pie crust with water. Fit top crust over apples and seal edge of pie. Cut or prick top of crust to allow steam to escape. Bake in a preheated 400° or 425° oven for 50–60 minutes.   SERVES 6

APPLESAUCE CAKE

From Senator Byrd

2½ cups all-purpose flour	½ teaspoon allspice
2 cups sugar	½ cup soft butter
¼ teaspoon baking powder	½ cup water
1½ teaspoons baking soda	1½ cups Byrd Applesauce
1 teaspoon salt	2 eggs
¾ teaspoon cinnamon	½ cup chopped nuts
½ teaspoon cloves	1 cup raisins, chopped

Sift together flour, sugar, baking powder, baking soda, salt, and spices. Add soft butter, water, and applesauce. Beat about 2 minutes. Add eggs and beat 2 minutes longer. Stir in chopped nuts and raisins. Pour into 13×9-inch oblong pan which has been greased and floured. Bake in a preheated 350° oven for 45–50 minutes.   SERVES 12

AUTHOR'S NOTE: To make applesauce (1½ cups): Wash, core, and quarter 6–8 tart apples. Add ¼ cup water. Cover and cook until soft, stirring occasionally. Press through sieve or food mill.

APPLE CRISP

From Senator Byrd

6 cups cornflakes	1 teaspoon cinnamon
1 cup melted butter	2 tablespoons butter
1 cup sugar	
4 cups sliced Byrd apples (Rome, York, Stayman)	

Roll cornflakes into fine crumbs. Mix melted butter with ¼ cup of the sugar and mix with crumbs. Set aside ½ of this mixture. Press the remaining ½ evenly over bottom and sides of a 9-inch pie plate.

Wash, pare, core, and slice apples and fill pastry shell. Sprinkle with remaining ¾ cup sugar and with cinnamon. Dot with butter. Sprinkle with remaining crumb mixture.

Bake in a preheated 350° oven for ½ hour. Reduce heat to 300° and bake until apples are tender (about an additional ½ hour). Serve warm with cream.   SERVES 6

CHARLOTTE MALAKOFF

From Dan Schorr

This is an elegant cream served in a mold with fresh fruit and whipped cream.

24–30 ladyfingers
½ cup orange liqueur
½ pound sweet butter
1 cup sugar
¼ teaspoon almond extract

1⅓ cups ground (almost
    powdered) unsalted almonds
2 cups chilled whipped cream
1 quart fresh fruit (e.g.,
    strawberries)

Line a 2-quart (high, not shallow) mold with ladyfingers, which first have been dipped into a shallow bowl containing ¼ cup of the orange liqueur diluted with 2 tablespoons water. The ladyfingers should be sticking up around sides of bowl. The liqueur will cause them to stick to the sides and keep their place.

Cream together butter and sugar for 5 minutes. Beat in the remaining ¼ cup orange liqueur and almond extract. Beat for a few minutes. Beat in the ground almonds.

Put about ⅓ of this mixture into the mold containing ladyfingers. Put in a layer of fruit, a layer of whipped cream, then a layer of ladyfingers. Repeat layers. If there are not enough layers to come to top of mold, trim off ladyfingers. Cover dish with waxed paper. Place lid or plate over mold and refrigerate overnight if possible. If you use a ring mold, it is lovely to fill the indentation with fresh fruit and top all with whipped cream.   SERVES 8

TOM McINTYRE

Senator from New Hampshire

Senator Tom McIntyre is New Hampshire's first Democratic senator in twenty-four years.

The self-styled moderate is a graduate of Dartmouth and Boston University Law School. He served as a major in the Army until 1946.

Early headlines about Senator McIntyre called attention to his personal trip to Alabama to investigate for himself facts surrounding the murder of civil rights marcher Viola Liuzzo.

He is known for speaking out on unpopular issues: He voted in 1969 to block the Safeguard antiballistic missile system and in 1970 he urged breakup of chain-owned news media.

The senator admits he has a sweet tooth and shares his family's recipe for Chocolate Steamed Pudding with sauce.

"This recipe dates way back to my early childhood and the real secret to this dessert is the sauce. I have seen other versions of Chocolate Steamed Pudding involving hard sauces, etc., but this one is my real treat!"

CHOCOLATE STEAMED PUDDING

From Senator McIntyre

2 ounces chocolate	*1 cup all-purpose flour*
1 tablespoon butter	*1 teaspoon baking powder*
½ cup sugar	*⅛ teaspoon salt*
1 egg	*½ cup milk*
1 teaspoon vanilla extract	

Melt chocolate and butter. Combine sugar and egg and beat until creamy. Add vanilla. Sift together flour, baking powder, and salt. Add the sifted ingredients alternately with milk. Beat the batter until it is smooth and pour into greased pudding mold (1-pound coffee can with cover will suffice). Steam for 1 hour.

SERVES 6

SENATOR MCINTYRE'S FAVORITE SAUCE

3 cups milk

½ cup confectioners' sugar

½ tablespoon butter

1½ teaspoons vanilla extract

Heat milk, sugar, and butter until very hot (do not boil). Add vanilla. Pour over room temperature pudding and serve immediately.

AUTHOR'S NOTE: There are several ways to steam a pudding. The pudding can be put into individual cups or molds (fill any mold you use only ⅔ full). The cups should be greased and when filled covered with plastic wrap, then put into a pan of hot water in a 350° oven.

Or the old-fashioned but more foolproof way is to put the pudding into the coffee can as Senator McIntyre suggests, or into smaller tin cans with tight covers, such as baking powder cans. Put the filled and covered cans on a rack in a kettle of boiling water. Keep the water boiling gently and add more boiling water during cooking time, making sure that only ½ the mold is immersed all the time.

TED STEVENS

Senator from Alaska

Senator Ted Stevens of Alaska has lived in Indiana, California, Massachusetts, China, and of course Alaska and Washington, D.C. He has held many interesting jobs including assistant minority leader of the Senate and assistant Secretary of the Interior.

He likes to cook when he has time and when his wife, Anne (who manages five children and a business of her own), does the preliminary preparation.

When Ted Stevens gets in the kitchen it is often to put together a menu of

Sable Fish (Alaskan, also called black cod)

Rice

Rolls

Tossed Salad

Dry White Wine

Chocolate Fondue

"I got the recipe for Chocolate Fondue while attending a Law of the Seas Conference in Switzerland. Senator Fritz Hollings (S.C.) was also a member of the delegation. His wife and mine had dinner with us one evening at a restaurant that specialized in fondue. After cheese fondue, beef fondue, and what have you, Hollings and I declined Chocolate Fondue. According to our wives when their fondue arrived we pushed their forks aside (as they attempted to dip in) and argued over who was getting the most Chocolate Fondue."

CHOCOLATE FONDUE

From Senator Stevens

Melt several bars Swiss chocolate in fondue pot. Have ready dishes of fresh fruit such as bananas, oranges, apples, grapes. Each guest is given a plate and fondue fork and helps himself, dipping the fruit in the chocolate.   SERVES 4

ITALIAN RAISIN LOAF CAKE WITH ICE CREAM (Panettone with Ice Cream)

From Embassy of Italy

Another special Italian cake dessert is made with Panettone, which is a rich, raisin bread kind of cake, usually sold in Italy at Christmastime.

The loaf is scooped out (reserve the excess) and filled with vanilla ice cream, whipped cream, and small cubes of the cake that have been scooped out. The dessert should then be frozen, but not rock-solid, and sliced.   MAKES 1 LOAF

AUTHOR'S NOTE: You can use a loaf of good unsliced raisin bread and sprinkle the cavity with confectioners' sugar and a few drops of anisette before filling with ice cream.

SICILIAN CAKE (Cassata Alla Siciliana)

From Embassy of Italy

1½ heaping cups ricotta (Italians recommend Fierro or Di Magio brands for American cooks)
1 cup confectioners' sugar
1 teaspoon vanilla extract
1½ ounces sweet liqueur, such as maraschino liqueur

2 1-ounce squares baking chocolate, broken into small pieces
½ cup candied fruits (mixed candied citrus fruit peel)
1 sponge cake, cut into 1-inch slices

Mix ricotta with confectioners' sugar and vanilla. Work well with wooden spoon, i.e., cream it together. Add liqueur (any kind of sweet liqueur you have on hand will do). When the mixture is soft, stir in small pieces of chocolate and the chopped, candied fruits.

Line a small square cake pan (8×8 inches is fine) with waxed paper, then line the pan on bottom and sides with slices of sponge cake. It is also a good idea to sprinkle a few drops of the liqueur on the waxed paper before laying in slices of cake. When the pan is lined with cake slices, it will be as a box made of cake. Spread the cheese-sugar mixture on the cake. Close the top of the cake "box" with more slices of cake, which will complete the preparation. Refrigerate awhile, but do not freeze. Unmold the cake, slice it, and serve. It is both beautiful and delicious. SERVES 8

ITALIAN ICE CREAM

From Embassy of Italy

2 eggs, lightly beaten
2 tablespoons sugar
Vanilla extract to taste (1 or 2 teaspoons)

1 cup heavy cream, whipped

Cream together eggs, sugar, and vanilla. Put in double boiler and stir constantly with whisk or wooden spoon. It will gradually thicken (about 7 minutes) over the hot water. Remove from fire and stir gently for 15 minutes until cool. When cool, fold in whipped cream. Put in refrigerator ice tray, stirring once or twice, and freeze for about 3 hours. The ice cream will be creamy, not hard. SERVES 4

CHOCOLATE MOUSSE

From Clifton Daniel

4 eggs, separated
¾ cup sugar
¼ cup orange liqueur
6 1-ounce squares semisweet baking
   chocolate

4 tablespoons strong coffee
1½ sticks sweet butter, softened
Pinch salt
1 tablespoon granulated sugar
Whipped cream

Beat together egg yolks and ¾ cup sugar. Beat in liqueur. Put mixing bowl over not quite simmering hot water and continue beating for 3 or 4 minutes. Then beat over cold water for same amount of time. Mixture, when cooled, should have consistency of mayonnaise.

Melt chocolate with coffee over hot water. Remove from heat and beat in butter, a little at a time, to make a smooth cream. Beat the chocolate into egg yolks and sugar.

Beat egg whites, with pinch salt, until soft peaks are formed. Sprinkle on 1 tablespoon sugar and beat until stiff peaks can be formed. Stir ¼ of the egg whites into the chocolate mixture. Fold in the rest. Put in individual serving cup-type dishes or pot de crème pots or into a serving dish and refrigerate for 2 hours or overnight, if possible. Serve with whipped cream.　　　SERVES 6

WILLIAM RICE

Columnist, the Washington Post

William Rice has been a writer for the Washington *Post* from the early sixties to present with two years off to travel in Europe. He spent most of this time in France, where he studied languages and food, attended the Cordon Bleu cooking school, and worked in the kitchens of various European hotels and restaurants. Bill is a bachelor and was able to chuck job and possessions and do his cooking thing for two years.

Bill cooks and entertains at home. He particularly likes vegetables and is not very interested in desserts. He is happy to have fruit and cheese, instead. However, if dessert is served, it is often his delicious Caramel Mousse. Also, "a light dessert should be accompanied by a good sauterne."

"More men are cooking and talking about it," he says, "because America's food tastes have been upgraded in the last ten years. We are being educated about foods, particularly foreign food, in newspapers' food pages and women's magazines. And because soaring food prices have caused us to think more about food and ways to prepare it so that our meals will be more interesting and economical. If we are to have a delicious meal from inexpensive meat cuts, or no meat, as is standard diet in many countries, we must learn how to prepare something other than a steak or a chop."

Bill is tall and slim and jogs daily to offset the cooking and dining that are part of his job—he tests each recipe before it is printed in the Washington *Post*.

CARAMEL MOUSSE

From William Rice

⅞ *cup* (*14 tablespoons*) *sugar*	6 *eggs, separated*
2 *envelopes unflavored gelatin*	¼ *teaspoon vanilla extract*
2 *cups milk*	2 *teaspoons strong coffee*

Pour ½ cup sugar in a heavy saucepan with ¼ cup water. Melt and continue cooking (do not stir after sugar has dissolved) until sugar's color deepens and it begins to caramelize. Off the heat add ¼ cup warm water (it will sizzle) and continue to cook. Stir with a wooden spoon until mixture is liquid. Set aside to cool.

Heat milk with remaining sugar.

Soften gelatin in ¼ cup cold water.

Stir egg yolks into a bowl, pour in some warm milk, stir, then return milk mixture to pan and stir continually over heat to form a custard that will coat the back of a spoon. Off the heat stir in gelatin and vanilla. Cool.

Mix cool caramel with custard and coffee in a metal bowl. Place in a larger bowl, partially filled with ice and water. Stir occasionally, while beating stiff 4 egg whites (of the 6 eggs used, discard 2 of the whites). As custard begins to set, gently mix in egg whites. Pour into a serving bowl and chill in refrigerator 2 or 3 hours or overnight.   SERVES 8

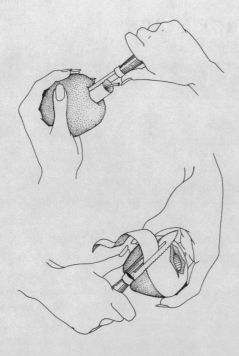

UPSIDE-DOWN APPLE TARTE (Tarte Tatin)

FILLING:
Sugar for covering bottom of pan
9 or 10 apples, peeled and thickly
  sliced
¼ pound butter (approximately)
⅔ cup sugar

PASTRY:
2½ cups all-purpose flour
½ cup butter
1 egg
⅓ cup cold water
2 tablespoons sugar
½ teaspoon salt

Choose a round pie pan or square deep baking dish. Sprinkle sugar about ¼ inch thick in bottom of pan. Arrange apples on top of sugar. Generously dot apples with chunks of butter. Sprinkle remaining ⅔ cup sugar over apples. Cover with short pastry and bake in a preheated 350° oven for about 45 minutes, until sugar is well caramelized and apples are tender.

Flip the tarte out on a cookie sheet, pastry side down, until the caramelized sugar runs down into apples; then flip the tarte over into serving dish so that the pastry is on top. Serve warm.

To prepare the *pastry:* Put flour in bowl, make a well, and add remaining ingredients. Work them all together slowly, handling as little as possible. Knead, sparingly, until dough forms a ball. Refrigerate a few hours. Roll out in usual pastry-rolling manner. SERVES 6

This is not the recipe of Sans Souci's Paul DeLisle, but the dessert is one of his favorites.

CARAMELIZED ORANGE SLICES

From Sans Souci Restaurant

  2 large oranges
  1 cup sugar
  2 tablespoons butter

Cut oranges in thin round slices, but do not peel.

Warm the sugar slowly, while stirring over direct heat until it melts. As sugar begins to melt, add the butter.

Stir steadily until a caramelly syrup forms in pan (I keep taking the pan off and on the fire), but take care to remove from fire as soon as there is syrup, as it will harden in the pan.

Dip the orange slices into the syrup and allow to cool on a rack or waxed paper.   SERVES 4

HENRY JACKSON

Senator from Washington

They say Senator Henry Jackson got the nickname "Scoop" because as a boy he delivered newspapers without a mistake or complaint. He learned the value of hard work and long hours as a youngster and today believes more than ever in this solid virtue. Unfortunately, along with the Puritan work ethic which is his own, he has been described by reporters as earnest, square, and somewhat humorless. "Slow to reach a decision, Jackson gains a kind of Old Testament certitude once he thinks something through," said a *New York Times Magazine* article.

But his constituents have returned him to the Congress for nearly four decades. He is one of the most powerful men in Washington, D.C., as chairman of the Senate's Energy and Natural Resources Committee and a member of Armed Services, Governmental Affairs, and Joint Committee on Atomic Energy.

Scoop Jackson aspires to the presidency regularly. Increasingly, the candidates and their wives are forced to publicize their opinions on everything. In the New York *Times* on April 12, 1976, reporter Klemesrud quoted Mrs. Jackson:

"More is expected of wives this year than at any other time in a Presidental campaign. We all discuss cerebral things. In fact I've only gotten one question about fashion, and that was from a man, and the only recipe request came to 'Scoop.'

"I think it's all because of Watergate and the women's movement."

Scoop Jackson answered my recipe request with Nordic Loaf Cake. The senator's parents were born in Norway and the cake is a family specialty. It needs time, both to assemble the ingredients and to prepare. It is worth the trouble.

NORDIC LOAF CAKE

From Senator Jackson

¾ cup blanched almonds, finely chopped (not ground)
3 cups all-purpose flour
1 tablespoon plus 1 teaspoon baking powder
½ teaspoon salt
2 cups heavy cream
2 teaspoons vanilla extract
½ teaspoon almond flavoring

2 cups sugar
4 eggs
¾ cup pignoli nuts (pine nuts) (almonds may be substituted)

GLAZE:
⅓ cup kirsch, warmed
⅓ cup sugar

Butter heavily 2 9×5-inch loaf pans. Coat the sides and bottom of each pan with finely chopped almonds.

Sift together flour, baking powder, and salt and set aside.

Whip cream in the large bowl of an electric mixer until it holds a shape. Add vanilla, almond flavoring, and sugar. Beat in the eggs 1 at a time. At the lowest speed, stir in the dry ingredients. Pour about ¼ of the batter into each pan. Sprinkle each with about 2 tablespoons pignolias. Cover evenly with the remaining batter. Smooth the tops. Sprinkle with the remaining nuts.

Bake in a preheated 350° oven for 1 hour or until the cakes test done. Remove from the oven and brush with the glaze made by mixing kirsch and sugar together. Let the cakes cool in the pans.

MAKES 2 loaves: SERVES 9

BANANA ICE CREAM WITH SOUR CREAM

From the Carl Bernsteins, who got it from Mike Nichols

4 bananas
4 peaches
4 cups sugar

4 cups sour cream
½ jigger Myers's rum (optional—
  Nora's addition)

Blend bananas, peaches, and sugar. Fold in cream and rum. Freeze in ice cream freezer or refrigerator.   SERVES 12–14

AUTHOR'S NOTE: I often take the liberty of reducing the amount of sugar in a recipe when it seems excessive.

CHEESECAKE

From the home of Tom Wicker

This is an old Russian Jewish recipe. It was adapted by Mary Rose Pratter to cream cheese and an electric beater.

3 8-ounce packages cream cheese
¼ cup all-purpose flour
1 cup sour cream

1 cup sugar
3 eggs, separated

Put cream cheese, flour, sour cream, sugar, and egg yolks in a mixing bowl. Beat with electric beater for ½ hour at medium speed. Remove batter. Beat egg whites separately until stiff and fold into cheese mixture.

CHEESECAKE GRAHAM CRACKER CRUST

2 cups graham cracker crumbs
½ cup melted butter

¼ cup brown or white sugar

Mix ingredients together and line by pressing mixture with hands the bottom of a 10×12-inch cake tin (pan with releasable sides is best). Or use angel food cake pan. Pour batter (including egg whites) into cake pan. Bake in a preheated 300° oven for 45 minutes. If you wish, spoon cherry pie filling over top and bake 15 minutes more. Take care cherries don't fall to bottom. Let cheesecake stand at room temperature for ½ hour; then refrigerate for ½ day or longer before serving.   SERVES 8

AUTHOR'S NOTE: Best cheesecake I have ever eaten.

AMBROSIA

From Representative Montgomery

4 oranges
1 8-ounce can crushed pineapple, drained, or 1 cup fresh pineapple, mashed
1 fresh coconut, grated (about 2 cups)

1 6-ounce bottle maraschino cherries, drained
Sugar to taste

Peel oranges, section, and remove white covering. Cut into pieces. Combine all ingredients and place in refrigerator to chill.   SERVES 6

AUTHOR'S NOTE: Even though it is more trouble, I always use fresh pineapple and fresh coconut when making this dish. The result is worth it!

DESSERTS   **223**

BOURBON COFFEE ICE CREAM

From Representative Montgomery

*1 quart good vanilla ice cream (or
make your own)
¼ cup Bourbon*

*2 tablespoons instant coffee powder
½ cup toasted almonds, broken up*

Let ice cream soften at room temperature. When it is soft enough to be worked, add the remaining ingredients and work in well. Return to freezer and let harden.

If you make your own ice cream, add Bourbon and coffee to your own stock or custard before freezing (if you are making more than 1 quart, increase the amounts proportionately). Add toasted almonds to the mixture in the freezer after it has begun to stiffen. This will keep the almonds crisp.   SERVES 4

AUTHOR'S NOTE: For those who like the taste of alcoholic beverages in their food, this is an agreeable variation of ice cream. I happen to like good ice cream in its natural form.

JOE L. ALLBRITTON

Publisher of the Washington Star

Joe L. Allbritton is a Texas millionaire, banker, board chairman, and owner of the Washington *Star*. He is casual and friendly, attentive to his wife, Barbara.

Joe said that although he couldn't cook, he makes coffee for his wife, Barbara, each morning. They remember being asked at a Texas party to give a recipe. Barbara's mother was nearby. She and Joe laughed and answered, "Barbara will tell you how to make chop suey—that is her one recipe." Their "Chinese" dish is not offered, but their ice cream is excellent, and it is the Texan's favorite dessert.

ICE CREAM

From Joe Allbritton

¾ cup sugar
1 envelope unflavored gelatin
2 cups milk
4 eggs, separated
¼ teaspoon salt

1 teaspoon vanilla extract
Dash cream of tartar
1 pint heavy cream
1–2 cups fresh mashed fruit
(optional)

Mix sugar and gelatin in top of double boiler. Add milk and heat and cook over boiling water for 5 minutes.

Beat egg yolks in large bowl. Add milk mixture to the egg yolks a little at a time. Return mixture to top of double boiler and cook until mixture becomes a soft custard and will coat spoon. Add salt and vanilla.

Beat egg whites and add cream of tartar. Continue to beat until stiff. Whip cream. Add egg whites to cooked milk mixture. Add whipped cream to mixture.

Put mixture in freezer. Put layer of ice then layer of ice cream salt around freezer cannister, alternating until bucket is filled and ending with layer of ice. Freeze until mixture is very soft. As ice melts in bucket, add more ice and salt in layers.   MAKES 1½ QUARTS

WHEN ADDING MASHED FRUIT:

Add 1–2 cups of any sugared (not heavily) mashed fresh fruit. Continue to freeze until firm. When firm, remove dasher and replace cover, being careful not to get ice or salt in container. Drain off water and pack with additional ice and salt. Cover with newspaper and leave for 15 minutes or longer.

PINEAPPLE MERINGUE TART

From the home of Ambassador Keeley

1 1-pound 4-ounce can crushed
    pineapple
4 egg whites
1 cup sugar
½ cup blanched almonds, chopped
Pinch cream of tartar

FILLING:
1 cup heavy cream
3 tablespoons milk
Confectioners' sugar

Boil pineapple with its juice in a saucepan until the juice is gone. Cool. Beat egg whites until stiff and add sugar, bit by bit, and chopped almonds. Spread on waxed paper on 2 insides of tart (pie) pans, or spread into rounds on flat cookie sheet. "Dry" in the oven at 300° for about 1½ hours until crisp.

Whip cream and milk (add milk toward end of whipping) until thick. Use ⅔ of this mixture to sandwich the meringue disks together along with most of the pineapple. Dust the tart with confectioners' sugar put through a sieve. Spread the remaining whipped cream and pineapple on top as decoration. Refrigerate until serving time.   SERVES 6

SOUR CREAM FUDGE CAKE

*From Craig Claiborne**

2 cups sifted cake flour
1½ cups sugar
1 teaspoon baking soda
1 teaspoon salt
⅓ cup shortening
1 cup sour cream

3 1-ounce squares unsweetened
    chocolate, melted
2 eggs
1 teaspoon vanilla extract
¼ cup hot water

Grease the bottom of a 13×9×1½-inch pan, line with waxed paper, and grease the paper.

Sift together flour, sugar, soda, and salt. Add shortening and sour cream and beat 2 minutes. Add chocolate, eggs, vanilla, and hot water and beat 2 minutes longer.

Turn the batter into the prepared pan and bake in a preheated 350° oven until the cake rebounds to the touch when pressed gently in the center, about 35 minutes.

Cool the cake in the pan 5 minutes. Turn out on a rack, remove the paper, and cool. Frost as desired. To serve, cut into squares.   SERVES 12

* From *The New York Times Cook Book,* by Craig Claiborne.

CHOCOLATE ROLL (Roule Marquis)

From Ambassador Rush

1 cup sugar
6 eggs, separated
⅔ cup cocoa
1½ tablespoons flour

3 cups whipped cream or crème
fraîche, lightly sweetened
Confectioners' sugar

Beat sugar and egg yolks until light and fluffy. Add cocoa and flour. Beat egg whites until stiff and fold into sugar mixture.

Butter a piece of parchment or waxed paper and place on baking sheet. Spread mixture ⅝ inch thick, 15 inches long, and 10 inches wide. Bake in a preheated 350° oven for about 18 minutes. Turn cake over onto clean dish towel. Remove paper and spread with whipped cream. Roll, using the dishtowel as a guide. Sprinkle with sugar. Refrigerate. To serve, cut in slices and serve with chocolate sauce.   SERVES 8

WILEY T. BUCHANAN, JR.

U. S. Ambassador

Wiley T. Buchanan, Jr., has been a banker, businessman, real estate investor, and presidential appointee to several foreign governments and Washington assignments. He was President Eisenhower's chief of protocol, ambassador to Luxembourg, and recently completed two years as ambassador to Austria.

The ambassador likes to talk about his various interests, particularly his lucrative affiliations in the business world. He is proud of being one of the founder-investors of the multimillion-dollar complex L'Enfant Plaza (home of the sprawling Department of Health, Education, and Welfare) in Washington, D.C. He owns several homes, one in an exclusive section of Washington, D.C., and a twenty-two-room "cottage" in Newport, Rhode Island, called Beaulieu, which once belonged to the Vanderbilts.

Wiley Buchanan in reminiscing about some of his experiences as chief of protocol remembered that Konrad Adenauer visited President Eisenhower at his Gettysburg farm. The President, the German Chancellor, and Buchanan all tried a TV dinner—they were just coming on the market. Ambassador Buchanan does not recommend TV dinners, but enjoys good plain food with emphasis on fresh vegetables. The Buchanans always maintain a garden wherever they are. An American vegetable garden was instituted in a corner of the official American residence which borders Vienna's famous Schönbrunn Palace.

As ambassador to Austria, the Buchanans entertain and are entertained constantly. They are proud of American food and often serve steaks, vegetables, and American ice cream. Sometimes the dessert is pineapple upside-down cake. This is a novelty for Austrians, who like its richness, particularly if it is topped with their adored *schlag*—lovely, fattening whipped cream.

They have contributed both American and European recipes.

PINEAPPLE UPSIDE-DOWN CAKE

From Ambassador Buchanan

1 cup all-purpose flour	*½ cup butter*
1 teaspoon baking powder	*¾ cup brown sugar*
3 eggs, separated	*8 or 10 pineapple rings, drained*
¾ cup granulated sugar	*8 or 10 maraschino cherries*
¼ cup pineapple juice	*Whipped cream*

Sift together flour and baking powder. Beat egg yolks and add granulated sugar, juice, and flour mixture. Beat egg whites until stiff and fold into sugar-flour mixture.

Melt butter in bottom of round 8- or 9-inch cake pan. Sprinkle brown sugar over this butter. Place pineapple rings in pan and insert a cherry in each hole of the rings. Pour the cake batter over all this and bake in a preheated 350° oven for about 45 minutes. Serve faintly warm, topped with whipped cream.

SERVES 6

LACE COOKIES

From Ambassador Buchanan

½ cup butter
½ cup flour
⅔ cup brown sugar

½ cup ground walnuts
½ cup oatmeal
½ cup light corn syrup

Heat butter slowly to the boiling point. Add remaining ingredients and mix well. Drop spoonfuls of the mixture on a buttered baking sheet and bake in a preheated 350° oven for 8–10 minutes.   MAKES ABOUT 3 DOZEN

BLACKBERRY PIE

From Senator Johnston

Senator Johnston does not have the traditional cake on his birthday, June 10. Instead, Mary Johnston makes blackberry pie, which he prefers to any kind of cake.

5 cups blackberries
1½ cups sugar
2 teaspoons grated lemon rind
¼ teaspoon salt
1 tablespoon lemon juice

4 tablespoons flour
1 9-inch pie shell
1 tablespoon butter
Dough for latticework crust

Stir all ingredients together until fruit is well coated. Pour into pie shell. Dot with butter. Cover with latticework crust. Bake in a preheated 450° oven for 10 minutes, then at 350° for 40 minutes or until brown. Cool and serve with scoop of vanilla ice cream on top.   SERVES 6

AUTHOR'S NOTE: This is a good method to memorize, as nearly all fresh fruit pie can be made the same way; i.e., mix fruit with sugar and flour, bake in hot oven a few minutes, then reduce heat.

MERINGUE CAKE

From the home of J. Carter Brown

1 teaspoon water
1 teaspoon white vinegar
1 teaspoon vanilla extract
¼ teaspoon baking powder
Pinch salt
1 cup sugar
3 egg whites

1 quart fresh strawberries,
raspberries, or peaches (reserve a
few to decorate)
½ ounce liqueur (Grand Marnier
or Quantro is good)
½ pint heavy cream

Combine water, vinegar, and vanilla. Combine baking powder, salt, and sugar. Whip egg whites and when they are hard, add sugar mixture alternately with the liquid mixture. Just dribble both mixtures into the whipped egg whites while you continue to whip. Spread the mixture into 3 1-inch-high rounds on a cookie sheet. Bake in a preheated 300° oven for ½ hour. Remove the meringues carefully from the pan and cool.

If using fresh strawberries, quarter them and sprinkle a little sugar on; peaches should be bite size also. If using frozen fruit, most of the syrup will have to be drained off. Spread a layer of fruit on 1 of the meringues, sprinkle a few drops of liqueur, then spread whipped cream.

Repeat all this with the second meringue and set it on the first meringue. After putting the third meringue on top the second meringue, cover it with whipped cream only, as you would frost a cake. Decorate with a few pieces of fruit and refrigerate for 3 or 4 hours before serving. Cut the cake with a hot, wet, very sharp knife. SERVES 6–8

ORANGE MARMALADE SOUFFLÉ

From the home of J. Carter Brown

8 egg whites
⅓ cup granulated sugar
4 large tablespoons Dundee orange
marmalade
Brandied peaches

SAUCE:
2 egg yolks
1 cup (approximately)
confectioners' sugar
1 cup heavy cream, whipped and
chilled

Beat egg whites, then gradually add granulated sugar. When it stands in peaks, fold in the marmalade. Turn mixture into top of a double boiler which has been well buttered and sugared (including the bottom of the lid), as soufflé will rise to the top.

Cook over boiling water for 40–50 minutes. Turn out on a round serving plate. Garnish with brandied peaches and serve with sauce.

To prepare the sauce: Beat 2 egg yolks and gradually beat in confectioners' sugar until mixture is stiff to beat. Just before serving, combine egg mixture and whipped cream and flavor with brandy.

Serve soufflé hot and sauce cold.   SERVES 6–8

BANANAS FLAMBÉ

From Senator Nelson

2 tablespoons butter
4 tablespoons brown sugar
2 firm bananas
Dash cinnamon

1 ounce orange liqueur
1 ounce rum or brandy
Vanilla ice cream (see note)

Mix butter and brown sugar in saucepan and cook over medium heat until caramelized. Cut bananas in quarters and add to brown sugar. Cook 2 minutes. Add cinnamon and liqueur and stir. Add rum or brandy to top of mixture. *Do not stir.* Light the mixture. Spoon over vanilla ice cream while flaming.

SERVES 6

AUTHOR'S NOTE: The ice cream should be the best quality available with high fat content (such as Louis Sherry or Breyer's).

BROWNIE PIE

From Senator Nelson

3 egg whites
Dash salt
¾ cup sugar
¾ cup fine chocolate wafer crumbs
½ cup chopped pecans

½ teaspoon vanilla extract
½ pint heavy cream, whipped and sweetened
1 1-ounce square unsweetened chocolate, shaved

Beat egg whites and salt to soft peaks. Gradually add sugar, beating until stiff peaks form. Fold in crumbs, nuts, and vanilla. Spread evenly in lightly buttered 9-inch pie plate. Bake in a preheated 325° oven for 35 minutes. Cool, then spread top with sweetened whipped cream. Chill for 3 or 4 hours. Trim with shaved chocolate. SERVES 6

Chapter 10

BEVERAGES

Not every interview for this cookbook yielded exciting recipes and interesting anecdotes about cooking. A conversation with a high-placed adviser to a recent president went like this:

"Do you like to cook?"

"No."

"Not even as a younger man, say when you were a bachelor?"

"No."

"Well, then, what is your favorite meal? What does your wife cook to please you?"

"I don't have a favorite dish. Food is not important to me."

"Perhaps when you entertain White House colleagues, you and your wife decide together on the menu?"

"No, food is something we don't discuss."

"What about your children? Do they like to cook anything special?"

"No, if anyone wants to eat, he just gets whatever happens to be in the kitchen, but food and cooking play no particular part in our lives."

The cookbook was nearly abandoned after this; but I managed to take comfort from the preface in Craig Claiborne's *New York Times Cook Book* (New York: Harper & Row, 1961):

"Cooking is at once one of the simplest and most gratifying of the arts, but to cook well one must love and respect food. . . . To enjoy the pleasures of the palate does not categorize a man either as a gourmand or glutton. As Dr. Samuel Johnson once observed, 'He who does not mind his belly will hardly mind anything else.'"

WILLIAM SAFIRE

Columnist, the New York Times

William Safire likes words, women, and work. He goes to his office in the New York *Times* Washington Bureau seven days a week. On weekends there are no children or secretaries to interrupt him and his most creative work is tapped out on the typewriter then. He talks to himself, laughs out loud, and paces and gesticulates alone in the large corner office that once held his colleague, Tom Wicker. Dialogue plays a major part in his writing and he often talks out the lines.

Bill Safire attended Syracuse University, did a tour of duty with the Army, went into public relations, formed his own firm, and for most of his life has been involved in politics and writing. He was a speechwriter for President Nixon for several years and left the White House in 1973 to become a New York *Times* columnist a few weeks before the Watergate scandal erupted. He has authored several books, including *Before the Fall,* on the Nixon presidency, and his first novel, *Full Disclosure,* a best seller, was published by Doubleday in 1977. These two works have earned him fame and much money, but words are his real love and he harbors secret pride for his word book, *Safire's Political Dictionary,* now in its third revision.

Usually the Safires entertain with large elegant dinners, sometimes as many as eighty seated at small tables. Helene Safire is responsible for these lovely parties. But Bill often grills a steak or prepares Steak Tartare (page 5) when only a few good friends are invited. Author and former CBS commentator Dan Schorr, Senator Bob Packwood, and London *Times* man Henry Brandon have enjoyed his raw beef.

Bill is pleasant and cheerful with an unfailing sense of humor. And he cooks the way he writes—with style and imagination. May Wine with endive and strawberries is his favorite: You drink the wine and eat the powerful "salad" that remains.

MAY WINE

From William Safire

1 quart chilled May wine
1 quart fresh strawberries, cut up
  (or frozen, drained)
4 Belgian endives, cut up

Pour chilled May wine over strawberries and endive. Allow to stand 1 or 2 hours. Serve with woodruff in wide champagne glasses so you can drink the wine and spoon up the "salad." This is refreshing for a summer luncheon.

SERVES 4.

AUTHOR'S NOTE: There is confusion about endive in America. These are the small (about 4 inches long) cone-shaped yellow-white vegetables one finds, usually in the packing box, in the supermarket.

JESSE HELMS

Senator from North Carolina

Senator Jesse Helms of North Carolina declined the request for a recipe: "I appreciate your interest but, frankly, this just isn't my cup of tea. I'll pass on this one."

Senator Helms's remark is discouraging, but in lieu of a discussion of food by him, we will talk tea.

Also discouraging is the decline in Britain of a great institution, afternoon tea. "Most people are just too busy rushing around these days to sit down for a full tea," admits a British official. This is generally true for the tea meal served in homes, but it still makes a handsome profit for hotels and teahouses.

Of course afternoon tea should include dainty, small sandwiches of perhaps watercress or cucumber, something very light; crusts should be removed. And if special guests are invited, scones and Scotch shortbread are delicious, unusual, fattening, and not difficult to make.

Tea is such a satisfying and refreshing pause and so much kinder to your health than coffee that dedicated drinkers will not be dissuaded. It is my persuasion that many Americans have never had properly brewed tea.

A GOOD CUP OF TEA

Rinse the teapot with boiling water to warm it. Put 1 teaspoon tea for each cup of tea needed and don't forget 1 for the pot. It is good to use 2 or 3 kinds of tea in 1 pot. I use some Twining's Earl Grey and Twining's Darjeeling. Sometimes I add a pinch of jasmine-flavored tea. After adding 1 cup *boiling* water for each teaspoon of tea, allow the tea to "steep" for 2 or 3 minutes. If the tea will be drunk immediately, it is not necessary to strain it into another hot teapot, but otherwise, do transfer it or it will become bitter as it steeps with the leaves.

It is nice to serve a pitcher of milk, and, of course, lemon wedges and sugar as a choice.

CHAUVINIST COFFEE

This is the name I apply to coffee with cream and sugar. Women usually drink black coffee and men usually say, Oh, I'll have just a little cream and a bit of sugar, as if it were easier to serve "a little" cream and sugar. Probably after years of serving men and children every meal and beverage, women have settled for less for themselves. In other words, a woman might like her coffee diluted, but this means getting out the milk carton and spooning the sugar, so she just learns to drink it black.

OLD-FASHIONED COCOA

If you have had any kind of struggle on a cold wintery night, for example with a balky car or a non-co-operative animal, or even sat through someone's dinner party in a cold dining room, there is nothing quite as calming and warming, when you finally reach home, as a good cup of *real* cocoa.

It isn't necessary to buy at the grocery store boxes or packets of somewhat perfumed chocolate mix. The best cocoa is a very simple blend of time and ingredients that are already in your cupboard.

½ cup sugar
½ cup water

½ cup noninstant cocoa powder
4 cups whole milk

Simmer sugar, water, and cocoa powder in a heavy saucepan over moderate heat, stirring until lumps are dissolved (about 3 minutes). Add milk to ingredients in pan, mix well, and bring slowly to simmer (about 5 minutes). Do not boil.

The result is cocoa that's chocolatey, sweet, and delicious. It takes about 8 minutes to make and costs only about 13¢ a serving—which is less than many instant cocoa mixes on the market.

Index

ALPHABETICAL LISTING OF CONTRIBUTORS

Index

RECIPES

Kathryn Wellde cooks, paints, and writes, and is a member of the Washington Bureau of the New York *Times*.

Her culinary talent gained a new dimension when, as a Foreign Service wife, she lived—and cooked—in Europe and the Middle East for thirteen years.

Entertaining was a necessity in the Foreign Service and experimentation with unusual and exotic foods became a challenge for Mrs. Wellde. As hostess to kings, princesses, ambassadors, and movie stars, she combined her natural hospitality and expertise in cooking to produce memorable dinner parties.

Mrs. Wellde studied art for many years and held one-person shows of her impressionistic paintings. She attended Tulane University and a cooking school for Viennese cooking in Germany. A widow, she has raised five children, two of whom are "pretty good cooks."

Russell Baker • Veal Scallopini • Chicken with Cream & Tarragon • Sautéed Scallops • Orar
with Basil & Tomato Sauce • Banana Ice Cream with Sour Cream • **William Brock** • Coun
Cold Avocado Soup • Special Graham Crackers • Meringue Cake • Orange Marmalade Souff
Cake • **Art Buchwald** • Lamb and Parsley Stew • **James Buckley** • Chicken Florentine
Applesauce Cake • Apple Crisp • **Jimmy Carter** • Peanut Soup • Eggplant Casserole • Japan
Chicken • **Craig Claiborne** • Meat and Spinach Loaf • Southern Fried Chicken • Coulibia
Turkey or Chicken in Cream • Cold Poached Salmon with Sauce Gribiche • Shrimp Fried
with Dill • **David Eisenhower** • Pan-fried Steak • Hot Fruit Salad • Cheese Grits • **John Gle**
Spaghetti • Stuffed Peppers • Pancakes with Beer & Blueberries • Danish Crescents • **Da**
Western Omelet • **Hubert Humphrey** • Beef Soup • **King Hussein** • Hummus al Tahini • B
Javits • Stuffed Cabbage • **Bennett Johnston** • Jambalaya • Green Peppers Stuffed wi
Pie • **Robert Keeley** • Chicken with Vermouth & Black Cherries • Mauritian Fish • Maurit
Chutney • Pineapple Meringue Tart • **Edward Koch** • Gazpacho • **Ned Kenworthy** • Saut
Broccoli Soufflé • **Paul Laxalt** • Basque Soup • **Anthony Lewis** • Granola • Carrot Brea
William Macomber • Shepherd's Pie • **Frank Mankiewicz** • Lentil Soup • **Mike Mansf**
Black-eyed Peas with Hog Jowl • Chicken Parmesan • Corn Pudding • Bacon-wrapped Bea
Bolognese • Green Spaghetti • Omelette aux Fines Herbes • **Gaylord Nelson** • Sour & Hot S
Walnuts • Bananas Flambé • Brownie Pie • Sweet and Sour Pork • **Robert Packwood** • Marina
James Reston • Mince • Eggs Fulton • **William Rice** • Grilled Kidneys & Sweetbreads
Veal Prince Orlov • Foil Pot Roast • Vichy Carrots • **Cliff Robertson** • Mussels • Clam Sauce
Zucchini • **Kenneth Rush** • Sea Bass with Fennel • Scallops en Brochettes • Brussels Fond
Sans Souci • Cold Rabbit in Terrine • Chicken from the Auge Valley • Fried Zucchini Flowe
Liver & Onions • Charlotte Malakoff • **Richard Schweiker** • Shrimp Dip • **Hugh Scott** •
• Bexar County Bean Casserole • Brioche • **Herbert Stein** • Leg of Lamb • Veal Shanks Ste
Herman Talmadge • Baked Country Cured Ham • Garlic Grits • Cucumber Mousse • **St**
Vorenberg • Hot Borscht • Cheese, Tomato, & Sour Cream Omelet • **Malcom Wallop** • Wyon
Bolognese • Polish Hunter's Stew • Chicken Tetrazzini • Chicken Breasts • Squaw Cor
Shrimp & Pesto Sauce for Spaghetti • Eggs Sardou • Hollandaise Sauce • Cheesecake • **Harr**
• Sautéed Scallops • Orange à l'Arabe • **Birch Bayh** • Green Bean Casserole • **Carl Bern**
• **William Brock** • Country Ham • Chicken & Brandy • Blender Hollandaise • **Edward Bro**
Orange Marmalade Soufflé • **Wiley Buchanan** • Chicken Piccata • Braised Endive • Lace Co
• Chicken Florentine • **Arthur Burns** • Veal Piccata • Omelet with Ham • **Harry Byrd** •
Casserole • Japanese Fruitcake • **John Chancellor** • Bacon, Lettuce & Tomato Salad • **Fra**
• Coulibiac of Salmon • French Brioche • Sour Cream Fudge Cake • **Clifton Daniel** • Veal w
Fried in Beer Batter • Zucchini Salad • Chocolate Mousse • **Antal Dorati** • Hungarian Goul
Glenn • Ham Loaf • **Barry Goldwater** • Black Walnut Stew • **Robert Griffin** • Meat Sau
Halberstam • Ham & Clam Chowder • Lamb in Marinade • Clay Pot Chicken • **H. R. Halde**
Ghanouj • Tabbouleh • Maqloobeh • Mensef • **Henry Jackson** • Nordic Loaf Cake • **J**
Squash & Shrimp • Eggplant Stuffed with Shrimp • Shrimp Creole • Okra & Tomato • Blackb
Lentils • Keeley's Egg Salad & Keeley's Fried Egg Sandwiches • Tomato Quiche • Maur
Flounder • Pasta with Clam Sauce • Bread • **Aaron Latham** • Ham & Cheese Poker Chip
Cream Cheese Frosting • **Robert McClory** • Swiss Cheese Fondue • Sour Milk Pancak
Butte Pasties • **Gillespie Montgomery** • Marinated Mushrooms • Lemon Pepper Melt
Spoon Bread • Ambrosia • Bourbon Coffee Ice Cream • **Patrick Moynihan** • Lasagna
• Scallions with Fried Pork • Grilled Leg of Lamb • Chinese Chicken Wings • Fried Chicken
Flank Steak • **William Proxmire** • Fruit Salad • **Dan Rather** • Brisket of Beef with S
Chicken with Wine & Vinegar • Green Sauce • Caramel Mousse • **Stewart Richardson** • R
Spaghetti • **Peter Rodino** • Escarole Soup • Veal with Marsala • Fried Italian Peppers • F
Chocolate Roll • **William Safire** • Steak Tartare • House Dressing for Green Salad • May W
Fried Zucchini Strips • Upside-Down Apple Tart • Caramelized Orange Slices • **Dan Scho**
Meat au Gratin • **Senate Dining Room** • Bean Soup • Beef Birds with Sauce • **William Sh**
• **Ted Stevens** • Poached Sable Fish • Chocolate Fondue • **Stuart Symington** • Bul Go
Thurmond • Crab Cakes • **John Tower** • Chili • **John Tunney** • Indonesian Rice • **Jam**
Steak Tartare • Boned Venison Sirloin • **Warren Weaver** • Liver Pâté Normandy • Eggp
Armenian Rice • **White House Chef** • Green Sauce • **Tom Wicker** • Pot-roasted Beef Lama
Williams • Shrimp Mousse • **Russell Baker** • Veal Scallopini • Chicken with Cream & Tarr